Moshe Guy Bursh
Daniel Shorkend

7 FOR 70

Moshe Guy Bursh
Daniel Shorkend

7 FOR 70

Torah Insights into the book of Devarim

JustFiction Edition

Imprint
Any brand names and product names mentioned in this book are subject to trademark, brand or patent protection and are trademarks or registered trademarks of their respective holders. The use of brand names, product names, common names, trade names, product descriptions etc. even without a particular marking in this work is in no way to be construed to mean that such names may be regarded as unrestricted in respect of trademark and brand protection legislation and could thus be used by anyone.

Cover image: www.ingimage.com

Publisher:
JustFiction! Edition
is a trademark of
International Book Market Service Ltd., member of OmniScriptum Publishing Group
17 Meldrum Street, Beau Bassin 71504, Mauritius
Printed at: see last page
ISBN: 978-620-0-49550-1

7 FOR 70

Torah Insights into the Book of Devarim

Moshe Guy Bursh, Sofer Stam and Dr Daniel Shorkend

This book is dedicated in loving memory of Tzvi Bursh and Tzvi (Harry) Shorkend, the respective grandfathers' of Moshe Guy Bursh and Daniel Shorkend respectively.

2

CONTENTS:

INTRODUCTION

The title of this small book refers to the changes that have taken place over the generations, namely that Torah must be spread among the 70 nations in order to publicise the 7 Noahide laws that are the basis for a just society in the Messianic era, the new age that is upon us. These laws are (this is taken from Chabad.org):

1. **Do not profane G-d's Oneness in any way.**

Acknowledge that there is a single G-d who cares about what we are doing and desires that we take care of His world.

2. **Do not curse your Creator.**

No matter how angry you may be, do not take it out verbally against your Creator.

3. **Do not murder.**

The value of human life cannot be measured. To destroy a single human life is to destroy the entire world—because, for that person, the world has ceased to exist. It follows that by sustaining a single human life, you are sustaining an entire universe.

4. **Do not eat a limb of a living animal.**

Respect the life of all G-d's creatures. As intelligent beings, we have a duty not to cause undue pain to other creatures.

5. Do not steal.

Whatever benefits you receive in this world, make sure that none of them are at the unfair expense of someone else.

6. Harness and channel the human libido.

Incest, adultery, rape and homosexual relations are forbidden.

The family unit is the foundation of human society. Sexuality is the fountain of life and so nothing is more holy than the sexual act. So too, when abused, nothing can be more debasing and destructive to the human being.

7. Establish courts of law and ensure justice in our world.

With every small act of justice, we are restoring harmony to our world, synchronizing it with a supernal order. That is why we must keep the laws established by our government for the country's stability and harmony.

7 and 70, that is 770 also refers to Chabad, the Chassidic expression of Orthodox Judaism that is the foundation of the authors' faith and path. Headed by the Rebbe, a man whose vision still has reverberations today following his passing in 1994, he has manged to reach Jews and non-Jews in awareness of God and the flowering of individual potential. The Chassidic philosophy which is one of no less than changing one's nature in the subordination or rather creation of emotions or "middot" based on thought; thought directed in the right way, activated by the power of the intellect or Chabad – "chochmah" (wisdom), "binah" (understanding) and "da'at" (knowledge).

Furthermore, many of the ideas contained herein are directly from the teachings of the sage, the Ba'al Shem Tov, the founder of chasisidism itself which taught that God is accessible to all; that love is the cornerstone and that the Messianic era or utopia will ultimately come about as God has promised.

Moreover, the title "7 for 70" is also a reference to the significance of the number 7 and 70 in terms of their correspondence with the letters' "zayin" and "ayin" respectively. "Zayin" refers to a realm above the 6 mundane days, that is it is the Shabbat and the "malchut" (kingship), the receptacle and fruition of the 6 days of work and is experienced on this day.

As well as a culmination, it is also an energy boost for the new week that is about to be. "Zayin" and 7 then refer to the mystical secret of a transcendent realm that invigorates the realm of the natural. "Ayin" and 70 refers to the 70 souls that went into Egypt and formed the basis for the Jewish people – 210 years later to be a large nation that made the Exodus. "Ayin" is also a reference to divine providence, the watchful eye that overseers all things. It is also the 70 languages and the 70 nations, and Israel is a kind of guiding soul for each nation so that if Israel does what it has to do the nations are elevated or conversely if the nations support Israel in the mission of monotheism and moral law and conscience and pool our spiritual as well as secular wisdom together with material wealth, then indeed the world can be transformed for the good.

Finally, there are 10 "parshas" (portion) in the book of Devarim (Nitzavim and Veyeilech are considered one). Now the phrase in Hebrew (David, Avdi) - David my servant - equals 100 (14 plus 86 = 100). This is the full complement of "sefirot" – Divine emanations or soul powers – that is, 10 sefirot within each one of 10 sefirot. The Messiah (Mashiach) is Moshe (345) plus David (14) which with the "Kollel" (an addition of 1 for the word) is equal to Mashiach (358) and thus the soul of Moshiach is a combination of two great lights, Moshe and David. Moshe recounts the Torah in this final book and the revealed word takes shape in this world in the ultimate sense which is the realm of Malchut (the final and 10th sefirah of kingship) and the domain of David, the King of Israel.

On a very basic level 7 refers to the visible light spectrum, the splintering of white light into seven colours. The structure of this book then is that each of the seven points for each parsha is a band of light as it were that refers back to that original light before being splintered through the prism, namely the focus of intellect on the holy text. And each nuance of the 7 visible colours (read: concepts) amplifies and assists the reader to somewhat grasp that divine light. This, in turn will enhance the readers' life.

CHAPTER 1

Devarim

אלה הדברים אשר דבר משה אל כל ישראל בעבר הירדן במדבר בערבה מול סוף בין פארן ובין (1
תפל ולבן וחצרת ודי זהב

"<u>These are the words</u> that Hashem spoke to all Israel, across the Jordan, in the wilderness, in the Plain, opposite (the Sea of Reeds), between Paran and Tophel and Laban, and Hazeroth and Di-zahab" (1:1).

"These are the words" – This convoluted phrase alludes to the idea that we have to know how to speak and to think and speak good things. We should avert our minds from bad thoughts about another which is so severe that it is akin to idolatry. In Zechariah (8: 17), the prophet lays emphasis on guarding one's thoughts as it says "...do not plot evil against each other, and do not love to swear falsely. I hate all this..." and in Tanya, (Iggaret HaKodesh – chapter 22), the Rebbe emphatically says that such negative thought patterns ought to be thrown out as it were as it says: "...one should push it away from his heart as smoke is driven away, as if it were an actual idolatrous thought". Since evil speech is compared to murder, incest and idolatry, how much more so evil thought, for thought is closer to the inner dimension of a person's soul

Deeper still, the initial letters of the first word – "elah" – aleph, lamed and heh ("these"), stand for something according to the commentaries (Ba'al HaTurim). This is followed by "hadiburim" meaning "these words". It can come to mean that the dust (afek) hints at evil speech (lashon harah), the first letters of which spell "elah". The Talmud teaches that one should be careful with one's speech and one should even guard against a single word. As it says in Pirke Avot (1:17) that Shimon his son said that he did not find anything better for his body than silence and that excessive talk brings on sin while silence protects his physical body. The sages want to reiterate that the main thing is not constant talk, but action and that if one simply engages in the former it causes sin. Chet or sin also means "miss" as in missing the target and so talk that is unmatched by action is such that one loses sight of one's goal and purpose.

2) ויהי בארבעים שנה בעשתי עשר חדש באחד לחדש דבר משה אל בני ישראל ככל אשר צוה יהוה אתו אלהם

"It was in the fortieth year, in the eleventh month, on the first of the month, when Moses spoke to the Children of Israel, according to everything that Hashem commanded them" (1:3).

Moses only rebuked Israel when he was close to his death. We learn this from the patriarch Jacob who rebuked his sons only just before his death. Similarly, Joshua did not rebuke Israel except immediately before his death and the same can be found with Samuel as well as David in relation to his son Solomon.

The Ba'al Shem Tov teaches that one should not harshly criticise one's friend and certainly not in anger. The greats of the past thus only criticised just before leaving the world. The Tanya (Likkutei Amarim, chapter 32) develops this further that while one can to an extent criticise one's friend, defined as one who follows the ways of Torah, for those not close, one should only have love and one should try bring him to Torah and mitzvot.

In fact, the moment one sits in judgement about others, one is in fact judging oneself. When one sees something wrong, it comes to you as a test in order to see how you will react. In fact, one should cultivate the habit of seeing the good, just as Rabbi Yitzchak of Berditivitch saw the good in others even in seeing a fellow eat on Yom Kippur he would assume a plausible reason why this person may have done so. In this way – by seeking out the good and giving the benefit of the doubt – one in effect changes reality towards the positive pole.

פנו   וסעו לכם ובאו הר האמרי ואל כל שבניו בערבה בהר ובשפלה ובנגב ובחוף הים ארץ הכנעני (3 והלבנון עד הנהר הגדול נהר פרת

"Turn yourselves and journey, and come to the mountain of the Amorite and to all its neighbours, in the plain, on the mountain, and in the lowland, and in the south, and at the seacoast: the land of the Canaanite, and the Lebanon, until the <u>great river</u>, the Euphrates river" (1:7).

The "great river" is great precisely because it is mentioned in connection with the Land of Israel. In a similar manner, Rashi continues that the "slave of a king is a king" and that to be in contact with one who is anointed is also anointed. That is, one's own power comes from the King and to therefore to attach oneself to His ministers – the holy Rebbe's and Tzaddikim – so one is empowered and connected above. This correlation between the greatness of the river since it is connected to the Land is similar to what is mentioned in Ychoshua (1:4) in reference to the "the big sea", that is, the Mediterranean. Now, obviously such a sea is of little expanse compared to the huge oceans of the world. However, since it is associated with the Land of Israel and marks its very holy borders, it is a "big" sea.

We see then that the ability of a person to keep good company and to learn from the wise and take counsel as well as keep and study books associated with Torah will, by implication connect one to the King. And thereby one's own inheritance is preserved and in effect, one himself becomes a king, if not over others then over himself.

הבו לכם אנשים חכמים ונבנים וידעים לשבטיכם ואשימם בראשיכם (4

"Provide for yourselves men who are wise and understanding and well known to your tribes, and I shall appoint them as your heads" (1:13).

The terms – "wise", "understanding" and "known"[1] - refer to the mental powers of the human being. Wisdom refers to the power to elicit ideas or to invent. It is a seminal point, the seed, the inspirational quality of an idea, a vision. Understanding on the other hand is

---

[1] The words for these mental faculties in Lashon Hakodesh, the Holy Tongue of Hebrew are chochmah, binah and da'at. The initials of each of these words spell Chabad, one arm of Chassidism in general.

the intellectual ability to take that flash of insight and develop it, logically building it in breadth, depth and height so that it truly takes shape beyond that initial point of revelation. Knowing is the co-joining of these powers, bringing the idea into reality, connecting with it conceptually so that an idea is born and in psychological terms it is the nexus between the intellectual realm and feelings. One might also say that whereas wisdom is associated with the male, with seed, so understanding is connected to the female principle, as she takes that seed and develops it in the womb, giving shape and form and complexity or detail to the initial insight, nourishing the idea so that it might grow into a "child".

Israel needs people with such powers: the ability to see, to have a general vision; the ability to analyse and give ideas full and detailed nuanced coherence and the ability to combine these mental processes and connect it to reality, that is to give birth to ideas in the form of completed projects, creations, constructions and so on. Moshe cannot do this alone. Others need to carry the weight, just as the Rebbe said that it is not he alone that can bring Mashiach, but every one of us, and the leaders of each generation need to motivate and inspire this vision and the mission of the nation and the creation of the Kingship of God here on earth.

Rashi[2] elucidates further the difference between the wise and those with understanding. He uses the analogy of the rich money-changer to describe the wise, while the latter use their intelligence to create business opportunities, expending effort to sell and execute his trade. In other words, wisdom consciousness is more passive – it receives from above in an open state of being, whereas understanding-consciousness is more logical, extrapolating one thing from another, dividing and assessing.

We want to be the one that understands…to change the world…demanded action…go out to the world…to bring Moshiach.

כי יהוה אלהיך ברכך בכל מעשה ידך ידע לכתך את המדבר הגדל הזה זה ארבעים שנה יהוה (5
אלהיך עמך לא חסרת דבר

"For Hashem, your God, has blessed you in all your handiwork: He knew your way in the great wilderness; this forty year (period) Hashem, your God, was with you; you did not lack a thing" (2:7).

In the great movement through the desert, there were 42 stops or stages. The Ba'al Shem Tov, the founder of Chassidus, explains that in each of us in our generation every day can actually experience a going out of Egypt and that one's life is a spiritual journey out of Egypt, wherein there are these 42 journeys – it is an analogy to one's time on earth. Just as we leave the narrow straits of Egypt, so each of us is birthed from a narrow or confined space into this world and the soul journey in life is such that we too need to constantly leave the materialistic pursuits of Egypt. The goal or final stop is the days of the Redemption wherein we can literally "smell" the truth. Within our soul of which there are five general levels, the highest or deepest is the "yechidah", the point of the Moshiach within. The Messiah is the general yechidah of everyone and if each us reveals that point of yechidah within then it will bring the general yechidah.

In order to access such a level, one should follow Rashi's commentary where he says that one should be grateful. It is an important practice to think of how God looks after one on even the most basic levels like food and shelter. These are ways God shows His care. In order to reflect on such perception, one should show oneself "rich", so as to give credence and thanks to the Almighty. Doing so is a kiddush Hashem – sanctifying the name of God. In so doing one can be described as an emissary of God.

רק נשיכם וטפכם ומקנכם ידעתי כי מקנה רב לכם ישבו בעריכם אשר נתתי לכם (6

"Only your wives, your small children, and your livestock – I know that you have abundant livestock – shall dwell in your cities that I have given you" (3:19).

Rashi comments that Hashem was speaking to the tribes of Reuven and Gad and that the East side of Jordan, would be for their cattle. Now Reuben and Gad had much cattle. Commentaries explain though that instead of eating from his produce, they were especially fond of the divine manna (divinely given food to the nation of Israel when they were in the desert for 40 years). Manna was special food, miraculous of course – it always looked the same and there was no waste having eaten of it. Also, the portion one was to be allotted was in accordance with his behaviour. If a person was righteous, the manna would be found at his doorstep and otherwise if not.

In effect, Reuven and Gad were so used to this spiritual food they did not want to enter the Land of Israel and work the Land and eat of its produce. Why the difficulty of ploughing and working when one can just enjoy the pleasure of the miraculous manna? Why have to deal with the physical world, when they could get a free lunch so to speak? They would rather just be simple God-fearing shepherds and find spiritual bliss alone within nature, just as Moses, Yaakov and David had been shepherds. In that time alone, one can gather one's thoughts and cultivate profound feelings of love and awe for the Almighty. We too should set aside time to be alone with God and should not be overly eager or immersed in the physical world.

Of course we do have to work the land of the Holy Land and we do have to be immersed within material pursuits to a degree – the Land of Israel is both a spiritual and physical home and requires that development must take place. Nevertheless, the children of Reuben and Gad suggest that we must equally have awareness of the miraculous and of the inherently spiritual nature of both ourselves and the task that is before us, namely raising consciousness towards an appreciation for more subtle ideas. However, the Torah deals with things of this world on a certain level of understanding, though the essence of a commandment[3] on higher spiritual levels, is expunged of such materiality.

7) The haftorah for this weeks portion is Isaiah (1:1-27). The last line reads: ציון במשפט
תפדה ושביה בצדקה

"Zion shall be redeemed with justice, and her returnees with righteousness".

"Mishpat" refers to those who deserve redemption as they did the spiritual work, whereas "returnees" refers to those who are considered captured (physically and spiritually) and will be redeemed through God's charity as it were.

In the days of the final redemption, unlike in Egypt when only a portion of the Jewish People came out of Egypt, will be such that all Jews will come out of the exile into the days of the

---

[3] The "commandments" are known as Mitzvot in Hebrew and are also more accurately translated as "connection".

Messiah and into the Holy Land. We will all receive God's blessings and each of us will have a part in the Great and final Exodus. As Micha says (7:15) and I am paraphrasing – the Final Redemption will be like the going out of Egypt, only more wonderful and miraculous. In Egypt we were enslaved 210 years while this exile has been 2000 years, so how much more extraordinary the Final Redemption will be!

CHAPTER 2

Va'etchanan

1) ואתחנן אל יהוה בעת ההוא לאמר

"I implored Hashem at that time, saying…" (3:23).

The first word "Vaetchanan" is the beginning of a deep plea ("imploring") by Moshe. In fact, he prayed 515 prayers to get into the Holy Land. The word itself has the numerical value of 515 which is equal to the word "tefillah" (prayer) and "shirah" (song).

The sages teach that there is nothing that stands in the way of prayer. Furthermore, that when one prays one must sing; one has to cultivate joy. It is an intimate bonding even deeper than the child for the parent. It has often been compared to the relationship between husband and wife.

2) There is an interesting gematria or conceptual equivocation. He found that אהבת לערך ואהבת את השם אלוהך equals כמוך אני השם

Namely 493. Rabbi Akiva said that the first part of this equation is really a summary or goal of all the Torah. Chassidut explains that to want to know God and serve Him, so one has to love the Jewish people. To love what one's beloved loves is to love the beloved. One has to emulate Hashem. Therefore, to the extent that one reaches out and loves, to the extent one has compassion and reserves criticism and sees the good in others, to that extent one is like God. God is not bent on destruction, judgement, hatred, vengeance and violence. Such a God is not the God of the Torah and where we appear to see God in such garments, it is an allusion to the human war against the evil inclination, the perpetual growth that one is called on to manifest in one's personal life.

Peace and love are the underlying intent, although justice and strength is called for. In this sense, one has to fight for peace. Such a paradox does not imply an insensitive, punitive, unloving God. God gives man the power to choose what to make of his life in this world. Such is the humility of God. Nevertheless, His ultimate will shall come to pass, irrespective of human error or actions. This is not to say one is indispensable, only that in truth there is nothing but God, however civilisation is said to progress or not. Loving one's fellow and loving God are the way we become partners with God in realizing the ultimate good and peace here on earth.

רק השמר לך ושמר נפשך מאד פן תשכח את הדברים אשר ראו עיניך ופן יסורו מלבבך כל ימי (3 חייך והודעתם לבניך ולבני בניך

"Only beware for yourself and greatly beware for your soul, lest you forget the things that your eyes have beheld and lest you remove (them) from your heart all the days of your life; and make them known to your children and your children's children" (4:9) and it continues in the next line that one shall teach them (ילמדון), a word that comes later in this sentence, only the vowelisation is slightly different.

Rashi explains that in the first instance it refers to oneself understanding the teachings of the Torah, while in the second usage, it refers to teaching others, linking in the process with the previous sentence, namely to teach one's children and even a generation beyond that, namely one's children's children. In fact, to the extent that one teaches others, so it is as if one has taught and helped create future generations.

The Rebbe explains and teaches that when one teaches others, not only does one have to learn alone in advance, but one's mind, brain and heart become a thousand times more spiritual, thus one's own learning in fact becomes easier and requires less time to cover more ground. What would ordinarily take a thousand hours to learn and absorn can be done so in an hour! Torah then is not only for one's own spiritual growth, but for the rectification and uplifting of the world and the transformation of darkness to light. This requires that Torah be taught in accordance with the Jewish tradition so that accurate interpretation and generations of commentary and explanation and interpretation is brought into the very air of the world at large, thus purifying it. To teach is the way to progress in the spiritual worlds.

ולא תחמד אשת רעך ולא תתאוה בית רעך שדהו ועבדו ואמתו שורו וחמרו וכל אשר לרעך (4

"And you shall not covet your fellow's wife, you shall not desire your fellow's house, his field and his slave and his maidservant, his ox and his donkey, and anything that belongs to your fellow" (5:18).

The ten commandments are recounted in this portion and here we read the tenth. The first two words is to want something that does not belong to you, to envy תחמד

Yet in the same sentence –תתאוה refers to not simply the desiring of what another has, but the kind of envy with the option, the calculation to in fact acquire such items by any means. Rabbi Yossi says in the Zohar that the Torah thus uses these different verbs in order to make a distinction in the meaning and intensity of the concept. Yet in both senses, one should stop oneself, whether in thought or deed, implying that one is to work on oneself both in terms of inner thought and feeling processes as well as actual behavioural output.

ובקשתם משם את יהוה אלהיך ומצאת כי תדרשנו בכל לבבך ובכל נפשך (5

"From there you will seek Hashem, your God, and you will find Him, if you search for Him with all your heart and all your soul" (4:29).

The first two words express a remoteness from God. Even if one is in a place remote from God, physically and/or psychologically – a place within or without void of Torah – even so, one can find Him where one is. The Rebbe develops this concept and explains that should one toil and struggle for the soul or within one's soul, one not only finds Hashem, but the revelation is not even proportionate to the effort. It is as if one has been given a great gift. It's like finding a diamond on the street. Sure, one might need the effort of sight and the strength to pick up the beautiful gem, but what is that compared to the lustre and brilliance, the shining wisdom embodied in the diamond, the Torah. Perhaps one walked around seemingly aimlessly and endlessly searching, but sooner rather than later, the shining luminosity of the diamond emerges and one's struggles and pain is all worth the "long and winding road".

A few lines later, we read:

אתה הראת לדעת כי יהוה הוא האלהים אין עוד מלבדו

"You have been shown to know that Hashem, He is the God! There is none beside Him!" (4:35).

To know that Hashem is Elohim and there is nothing else besides is very crucial and high meditative insight. The tetragrammaton refers to God as He reveals Himself as mercy in the world; Elohim to God as revealed in nature (the word for nature and Elohim have the same numerical value) and the idea that "there is nothing besides" is a very high level and the recognition that the world itself is "hevel" (as is the name of Caan in Genesis and "vanity of vanities" is the Song of Songs)- a mere nothingness, a little speck, but a puff of air, shadows and dust, a material embodiment of something more rarefied, something infinite and eternal compared to the dross, chaos and limitations of this world and those beyond it, howsoever they may be more spiritual or refined. In other words, the life of life cannot be defined or grasped, but is the very root and reality of all that apparently exists.

Furthermore, the Zohar reveals that Hashem gives of Himself in accordance with the capacity of the vessel to receive. One therefore needs to strengthen the vessel in order to contain and reveal that light. Such strengthening is achieved by following the dictates of the Torah in body and spirit. This means that one should direct the garments of the soul – thought, speech and action – in the ways of Torah. Then Hashem will grant the recipient light in a way that will be assimilated, understood, integrated and appropriately expressed. That is why great sages are living Torah scrolls and why we speak of the patriarchs and matriarchs as God's chariots, as were the prophets, judges and kings. Indeed our generation stands on the shoulders of giants having survived the ages made possible by the spiritual realization that God is in control and there is no other power that reigns.

6) אנכי יהוה אלהיך אשר הוצאתיך מארץ מצרים מבית עבדים

"I am Hashem your God, Who took you out of the land of Egypt, from the house of slaves" (5:6).

This powerful first commandments embeds the every structure of the Torah and can be envisages as a prymaid. The base is such the Torah is wide etc but measurable.

One stage higher, you come to tannach (THE Chumash, writings and prophets) which is a little more contracted.

Then further up, more narrow are the 10 commandments consisting of just 620 letters

Still more concentrated is the word "anochi", "I", the very essence of God.

Then there is the first letter – alef

And the final concentration of it all is the beginning of the letter alef itself – the point.

To spell this out: Each letter of this important first word comes to teach us something: Alef of "Anochi" (note …("I") – alef, nun, cuf and yud - refers to the Torah as "aruchah meeretz", as wider than the land (Job 11:9), that is that Torah is vast but yet measurable, within certain material parameters, partial to measurement and definite parameters; able to be grasped and ordered. The next level of concentrated wisdom or "tzimzum" (Divine self-restriction) is nun for "Nach" – the prophets and writings. The cuf is the chumash, the five books of Torah which is the very skeletal structure of everything around it, namely the oral law, the Talmud and the corpus of writings and commentaries and the concealed dimension, the kabbalah and esoteric wisdom. The yud is the chumash contracted further into the ten (yud) commandments which holds the kernel idea for the full spectrum of the 613 commandments or mitzvot. The next level is the very restriction and solidification of the ten commandments itself within the form of the Alef, the silent letter that is the basis for everything subsequent, for it is the Alufah shel olam, the master of the world and the highest point is the kutz, the little point of the yud that begins the alef and refers to the very essence of God that is given through Torah and that is an inheritance of Jacob. This inner point is the liminal point between spirituality and material being. It is the portal or gateway to the hidden things, the secrets that have yet to be revealed and is somewhat accessible still in the great works of the kabbalah.

And what is the very purpose of all this? For in the same sentence, an awareness of Torah is based on freedom, on breaking free of the shackles of Egypt. Egypt comes from the root (meitzar) meaning narrowness, constriction, potential stifled. By moving closer to Hashem's Torah we acquire freedom and are less likely to be slaves – slaves to society, to our drives and unconscious impulses and desires.

7) שמור את יום השבת לקדשו כאשר צוך יהוה אלהיך

ששת ימים תעבד ועשית כל מלאכתך

ויום השביעי שבת ליהוה אלהיך לא תעשה כל מלאכה אתה ובנך ובתך ועבדך ואמתך ושורך וחמרך וכל בהמתך(וגרך אשר בשעריך למען ינוח עבדך ואמתך כמוך)

"Guard the Sabbath to sanctify it, as Hashem, your God, commanded you" (5:12)

"Six days shall you work and do all your work" (5:13)

"But the seventh day is Sabbath to Hashem, your God; you shall not do any work – you and your son and your daughter and your slave and your maidservant and your ox and your donkey and your every animal, and your convert within your gates, in order that your slave and your maidservant may rest like you " (5:14).

Shabbat is a central concept in Judaism. All the days of the week we make the effort to prepare and work for the Sabbath. Then we arrive at the essence of the week. The Rebbe explains that there is a physical and spiritual dimension to Shabbat. Physically, one must have "oneg", pleasure in the Shabbat from her physical delights – the taste of food, sleep, drinks and so on. When the angels sees the beauty of Shabbat as the table is bedecked and the candles are lit, it too has to acquiesce and so there is peace on Shabbat. Then the week is blessed by her.

The Rebbe explains that the spiritual dimension of Shabbat is that it inspires the week to follow as one lives with the "parsha" that is to be read on Shabbat, thus vitalising the week with the holiness of Shabbat and then accepting that energy on the shabbat itself as it then flows into a new week and new spiritual cycle. That is to say, Torah is something lived, not simply of academic interest or some archaic tear of punishment or shadow self-concepts. Each day we remind ourselves that Shabbat approaches.. As we read "the first day...", "the second day..." and so on at the morning service each day of the week we count from and toward the holy shabbat and in the process draw light that can expel darkness or shadow beliefs. Through, as the Rebbe says, living with the "parsha", a meta-narrative, one's own life is infused with light: one is not a victim and one's true life journey is to grow, express and expand as a soul.

In this way, the Rebbe explains, what one learns during the week, both body (halachah – Jewish law) and soul (kabbalah, chassidut) will prepare one, for what one learns (in actual fact, not academically) through the experience of Shabbat. What this means, explains the Rebbe that now more than ever the secrets of the Torah are needed and need to spread to the most isolated places on earth so that the 70 nations and 70 languages hear the message and that therefore the secrets need to be conveyed in their language.

Shabbat is the state when a higher order is reached, while as we prepare for the redemption and the time will come when the nations help Israel and build, create and develop the earth so that the Messianic Era can be. In fact, the Rebbe writes the nations will be compelled (consciously rise up) to study lashon hakodesh (the Hebrew language). Meanwhile there is a little time and the secrets need to be disseminated – the employer is insistent and the day is late – as the Messianic Era suddenly dawns on us all. Then humanity will have become like a higher order organism and direct its energies to knowing God and being righteous.

CHAPTER 3

Eikev

והיה עקב תשמעון את המשפטים האלה ושמרתם ועשיתם אתם ושמר יהוה אלהיך לך את הברית (1
ואת החסד אשר נשבע לאבתיך

"And it will be because of your listening to these ordinances, and your observing and performing them; then Hashem your God, will safeguard for you the covenant and the kindness that He swore to your forefathers" (7:12).

"Eikev" here refers to the "heel". The heel is the lowest part of the body. It is also one of the least sensitive parts of the body; one can endure just about fire without causing severe pain compared to other parts of the body. The message for us is that Hashem and His Torah must penetrate to the very lowest points and depths both within an individual and within the world as a whole. His Light must be all-encompassing and effect all levels of existence, even the least sensitive aspects to the Godly. In that way His Way can be known and the sensation of His Presence revealed to all. In fact the halachah (Jewish law) discusses every detail and facet of life even matters pertaining to going to the toilet! This teaches that it is important in dealing with spiritual things to keep the body, environment and clothes clean and this therefore reflects and causes better thoughts (through learning, kabbalah, tzedakah) i.e. the soul dimension.

ויענך וירעבך ויאכלך את המן אשר לא ידעת ולא ידעון אבתיך למען הודיעך כי לא על הלחם לבדו (2
יחיה האדם כי על כל מוצא פי יהוה יחיה האדם

"He afflicted you and let you hunger, then He fed you the Manna (divine food) that you did not know, in order to make you know that not by bread alone does man live, rather by everything that emanates from the mouth of God does man live" (8:3).

Everything in the material universe has both a physical and spiritual dimension. It was difficult for the philosophers to understand how it is that man derives life and substance from food. In other words, since the lack of food separates the soul from the body, why is it then that food affects the soul since surely it is the body that enjoys the food?

Arizal, *Ha Ari Hakadosh* comes to explain that in fact since the world is built on words, namely the "speech" of Hashem, they are always present in the material object to which it enlivens. The words as such are the energy and life of that very thing (the word "davar" in Hebrew means both "thing" and "word").

Now, if we take food and say a blessing on it before and after consuming it, then we as it were "remind" God of the spiritual connection to or of that thing; its very energy and soul.

And that is why it says "not by bread alone", for it is the spiritual aspect of the food viz its "letters" (sparks) that through the corresponding blessing raises that thing up and by extension, the one that eats it, back to its source; a return of something back to the nothingness from which all emanates. This is achieved by blessing the food one eats, that which will be a part of his soul and blood, and extracting the holy sparks encumbered in course, dense material reality. (c.f. psalm 119 – sentence 89 – "forever, Hashem your words stands firm in heaven").

Ba'al Shem Tov further explains why in fact there are so many different kinds of foods. He explains that Hashem does so, because everyone has his sparks, so to speak that he has to sift, refine, fix and so there are numerous attractions. Each person is different and attracted to different and subjective delights and pleasures in order for that soul to redeem specific sparks. The Rebbe in Hayom Yom for gimmel (3rd) Elul, further adds that for those who believe in Divine Providence so Hashem matches each individual to the sparks he has to sift and refine and fix so that no soul comes to a place for no reason. One's task is to tap into this primeval agenda that was instituted from the very creation of the world and embrace this kind of hero-journey so that the soul might accomplish its task here during its sojourn on earth.

ארץ חטה ושערה וגפן ותאנה ורמון ארץ זית שמן ודבש (3

"a land of wheat, barley, grape, fig and pomegranate; a land of oil olives and honey" (8:8).

This sentence refers to the 7 species in the land of Israel. It is these species that ought to be blessed. A little further on the Torah says:

הטבה אשר נתן לך ואכלת ושבעת וברכת את יהוה אלהיך על הארץ

"You will eat and you will be satisfied and you will bless Hashem, your God, for the good land that He gives you" (8:10).

From here we learn as a Torah injunction that we have the mitzvah of Birkat HaMazon (thanking God after consuming bread). The rest of the before and after blessings were instituted later by the wise one's of the Torah down the ages ("chachamim" or sages and prophets between the first and second Temple era) and even if one ate an insufficient amount to be full. What we learn is that the earth belongs to God and we bless before eating to acknowledge as such, while we further learn that the enjoyment of it requires a blessing after partaking of food. This creates a consciousness of G-d, the ever-present Creator throughout the day as a number of blessings ought to be said.

המוליכך במדבר הגדל והנורא נחש שרף ועקרב וצמאון אשר)4

אין מים המוציא לך מים מצור החלמיש

"Who led you through the great and awesome wilderness – snake; fiery serpent, and scorpion, and thirst where there was no water – Who brings forth water for you from the rock of flint" (8:15).

The Rebbe writes in his analysis of the sentence that the various words "great"; "awesome"; "fiery serpent"; "scorpion"; "thirst"; "no water" and "rock of flint" refer to seven stages or rather 7 barriers toward spiritual fulfilment or reaching one's higher self and an accord, a bonding with God. These 7 stages remove a person from awareness of God distancing a person from the immanent Light and the special quality of Israel.

"Great" – this a reference to the idea that a person sees the world and its great nations with its pomp and power as being too large, whereas the Jewish world is puny by comparison. In simple terms one feels small and the nation of Israel as been insignificant.

"Awesome" – Here the person is fearful. He thinks that should he make changes in his life and observe the Mitzvot then what will others think of him; will he not be ostracized. He feels fearful and without strength to follow through.

"The snake and fiery serpent" refers to the passions for the world, the desire to engage in the pleasures of the world and his feelings or attractions toward the holy become limited and weak. His desires for materiality are greater than his wish for spiritual nourishment and holiness. His energy is thus diverted and misused.

"Scorpion" - here the person is weakened by his indifference and coldness. Its one thing to vigorously and passionately deny Torah and Mitzvot – in such a case at least he is fired up and the question of truth matters to him. But here, we have an individual who simply does not care for such matters; his heart and mind are cold. This is a serious problem and comparable to Israel's arch-enemy, namely Amalek, that force that weakens the inherent spirituality of the Children of Israel.

"Thirst" or tiredness is also terribly negative. It is a depressed energy, a lack of interest in life, tired by one's experiences and pain; a life without direction or a clear goal bereft of a disciplined regimen of self-growth, such as prayer and Torah study. Such sadness is contrary to an enlivened soul inspired by the presence of God or at least His incumbent redemption.

Lastly, the level of "no water" is a certain emptiness and one who does not even know he lacks Torah, so his thirst can never be satiated.

But there is a solution to these levels of degradation and this is hinted at the word "hard rock", namely החלמיש whose letters can be rearranged as למשיח, that is "to the Messiah". To the extent we can connect to the Messiah within - that spark of holiness - so one can generate a closeness to God and spiritual life or rather one where materiality is spiritualised and this can be accomplished through the study and practice of the Torah, thus overcoming the enemies enumerated above.

5)

ועתה ישראל מה יהוה אלהיך שאל מעמך כי אם ליראה את יהוה אלהיך ללכת בכל דרכיו ולאהבה אתו ולעבד את יהוה אלהיך בכל לבבך ובכל נפשך

"And now, Israel, what does Hashem, your God, ask of you but to fear Hashem, your God, to go in all His ways and to love Him, and to serve Hashem, your God, with all your heart and with all your soul" (10:12).

The word "Mah" – "what" - is used. The Zohar says what does a person ask of you? Surely, that what God asks of a person, namely to fear, to love, to serve is surely a terribly difficult and high level to attain. Nevertheless, the Zohar explains that should one pursue Torah as if it were a great treasure, then one will find it and come to these levels. It will then not appear as such an arduous task. When we get in touch with the point of Moses within us, the very deepest points within our souls, then it is easy in fact to achieve what Hashem demands of us.

"Mah" (what) has the same numerical value as Adam and Geulah (Redemption), that is – 45. And the redemption of man is both an individual and collective event or process. It is made possible with Moses's humility when he says we are but nothing (we are "what") and it is this self-effacing realization that is the very core and beginning of spiritual work and of becoming a Torah oneself.

עשה משפט יתום ואלמנה ואהב גר לתת לו לחם ושמלה (6

"Who carries out the judgement of orphan and widow, and loves the convert to give him bread and garment" (10:18).

Bread and clothes are not things one should take for granted. Rashi himself in his commentary writes that they are indeed crucially important and one should say thanks for such items. In fact, Ya'akov, our forefather, prayed for them and that Hashem should provide him with them.

Chassidus explains the spiritual intent around "bread" and "garment". The former refers to learning Torah and like food that it should be ingested and digested and become a very part of his blood as such. It should fill his being. This is "mamele kol Almin" (inner light). The latter refers to "Or Makif", the surrounding light, rather than within one's body and being. For garments surround the body and this refers to the Mitzvot in general that clothe the body in holiness when one is engaged in them.

The Torah then goes on to the commandment (or point of connection) to love the convert. A convert is one whose Godly soul is entrapped by its foreign body; the soul is even more in exile in the body than the Jew by birth. Yet, it is by Torah and Mitzvot that one connects back to the Source and free the soul to do its work in and through the body so that there should be redemption. Unlike other belief-systems, Judaism does not decry the body or argue that man is forever downcast in "original sin". No, the Righteous and the Torah itself is the elixir and the mechanism where the stain of Adam and Eve and subsequent generations have not removed God's presence or damned man in a lustful, dark body. There is a cure and the body is elevated in the process. Torah shall heal the world.

וכתבתם על מזוזות ביתך ובשעריך (7

"And you shall write them on your doorposts of your house and upon your gates" (11:20).

The Rebbe writes (Likkutai Sichot, book 19, Eikev) that Israel are the one sheep among 70 wolves (nations). Yet there are methods by which we protect ourselves. We have a system of self-defence.

Much suffering strangely is as a result of mezuzot that are not kosher or even completely absent. So, every Jewish house must have them in accordance with halachah – Jewish law. It brings life and safeguards us. In fact, the Zohar goes so far as to say that it protects us even as we linger far from it. The mezuzah acts not simply as a "bodyguard" in the home but extends its arc and radius of influence and power when that man or woman leaves their home and goes elsewhere in the outside world.

Deeper still, one should see Israel as "one man", one organic body so that each of us effect the other. Just as Israel was one when receiving the Torah, so one should identify with his brother, however different. By keeping mezuzot kosher we enhance our connection to one another and thence the health of the Jewish nation, the body as a whole.

CHAPTER 4

PARSHAS RE'EH

ראה אנכי נתן לפניכם היום ברכה וקללה (1

"See, I present before you today a blessing and a curse." (11:26)

"Anochi" or "I" is a very significant word. We find it used as the first word in the Ten Commandments. It hints at G-d Himself, higher even than the various names of G-d, since the "I" refers to essence preceding names and their descriptive limitations.

The deeper meaning here is that to "Re'eh" – to "see" – is to be aware of the presence of the essence of G-d in one's life – and it is on that basis that one will receive blessings. The Torah uses the word "lifnaichem" which has two meanings. It can mean "in front of you" and it can also mean "inside of you". One ought to feel the presence of G-d in both senses. Firstly, that G-d is in front of you implies He is available to you, that He leads you and one sees Him, so to speak as one moves forward in time, in life. The other sense, namely to perceive G-d "within oneself" is equally important. One who makes G-d a part of one's being suffusing a certain consciousness of G-d within one's world, one's very inner world of thoughts and feelings, is a fitting receptacle for G-d's blessings.

ושמחתם לפני יהוה אלהיכם אתם ובניכם ובנתיכם ועבדיכם ואמהתיכם והלוי אשר בשעריכם (2

"You shall rejoice before Hashem, your God: you, your sons and your daughters, your slaves and your maidservants, and the Levite who is in your cities".

"Rejoice" – This is a crucial concept in Torah and true service. That is, G-d wants us to be happy, we have to have joy, energy, enthusiasm, alacrity and that should encompass one's entire self and one's entire household. To the extent one can set G-d before one to light up one's path as intimated above, so one can both see the blessings in one's own life and even be a conduit to bless others.

Indeed, one can know that one is doing the right thing in the service of G-d to the extent that one is happy and joyous. Such positive energy or spirit gives one power and in fact, whatever one's difficulties, a solution is more likely to dawn on one if one cultivates this soul-power, while hardship is less likely to defeat one's spirit. The power of happiness, power, energy is

His presence (being in the right place), for one is in the right position no matter what one is doing. Unhappiness on the other hand is the inability to commune (communicate) with G-d "face to face" so to speak; it's as if one is looking for G-d, forever behind, out of place, rather than a connection with G-d such as one as immersed in His light and presence.

We therefore have an actual mitzvah to serve G-d with joy. But can we always be happy? Surely this is too difficult considering the pain and hardship of life? There is a story told of a chassid whose house burnt down, a fate suffered by others. But when the townsfolk were lamenting their fate, he was singing. Why? Is this not absurd? His response was that he is happy simply because he is a Jew and that is something that can never be burnt down, so to speak. And so he even danced for joy.

The lesson is that even when we suffer loss, even when we do not have what we need, happiness itself will generate a solution to our problems. The Rebbe said that one goes out of all one's troubles simply by being happy. As it says in Isaiah 55:12 – "You shall go out in joy and be lead in peace; the mountains and hills will burst into song before you, and all the trees of the field will clap their hands". Happiness breaks the limitations of one's nature. It is said to sweeten the "gevurot" (the judgements), so that what is bitter may be experienced as sweet. It cultivates a mind-set that everything is part of the plan, even that which appears to oppose goodness and blessing. This outlook may be termed a philosophy, a means whereby one can face life with strength and faith in God, the Creator.

רק חזק לבלתי אכל הדם כי הדם הוא הנפש ולא תאכל הנפש עם הבשר (3

"Only be strong not to eat the blood – for the blood, it the soul – and you shall not eat the soul with the meat"

Rashi mentions the Tanna, Rabbi Shimon ben Azzai that the attraction of eating blood is not strong, so that even more so, in that which is desirable and attractive, one should be scrupulous in observing the mitzvot and have the strength to exert oneself in carrying out all the commandments. Since even in a matter which hold little proclivity to transgress, one ought to be strong, how much more so in matters where the pull of the body and lusts is that much greater and more forceful.

Two lines further, the Torah reads:

לא תאכלנו למען ייטב לך ולבניך אחריך כי תעשה הישר בעיני יהוה

"You shall not eat it, in order that it be well with you and your children after you, when you do what is right in the eyes of Hashem"

Rashi further comments that since Hashem will give a reward – a salary so to speak – even and all the more so in matters which the soul does not desire, in fact disgusts and so abstains, how much more is this true in matters such as theft and sexual immorality which the animal soul may desire. Indeed, such reward will be greater the greater the test (and that's personal for each person) and it is not only for oneself but also one's descendants.

4) שמר ושמעת את כל הדברים האלה אשר אנכי מצוך למען ייטב לך ולבניך אחריך עד עולם כי תעשה הטוב והישר בעיני יהוה אלהיך

"Safeguard and listen to all these matters that I command you, in order that it be well with you and your children after you forever, when you do what is good and what is right in the eyes of Hashem, your God".

"All these matters" - that is to say, in the service of Hashem, one should strive to fulfil all the commandments and not simply what is convenient or appeals to one's reason. One cannot simply choose which commandments are suited and which simply not, rather than the sincere service and obedience to the giver of life, which entails following all His directives, even when the task does not appear to be simple and easy. Yet one should know to listen to God is for our own good; it is what is best for us and for the world – the logic of God is all-encompassing and He alone knows the mechanism or the tonic to both heal ourselves and the world as a whole. It is a logic that is supra-rational and those that wish to follow in its truth must do so wholeheartedly so as to do all the positive commands and refrain from the negative commands for *all* the mitzvot are important.

This, however need not be seen as an arduous task. Indeed, the founder of Chassidus, the Ba'al Shem Tov said that one must do the mitzvot with light, with a sense of beauty. In so doing it will be well in two respects as Rashi's commentary notes that "good" in the text refers to the fact that one shall be good in the eyes of Hashem and "right" refers to that one shall be good in the eyes of other people too. This is exemplified by many great Torah sages, such as the Chabad Rebbe, who spent many hours giving to the people even at an advanced age, rather than studying Torah, teaching that one has to be both in service of God and also make time for one's fellow man.

5) עשר תעשר את כל תבואת זרעך היצא השדה שנה שנה

"Tithe, you shall tithe the entire crop of your planting, the produce of the field, year by year" (14:22).

The simple meaning is that when one grows fruit and vegetables in the Holy Land, one must give a portion to the Cohanim (priests). The gemera in Ta'anit (page 9) learns further than one is enjoined to give 10 percent of one's profits as tzedakah (charity).

There is a general principle in the Torah that one should not test Hashem. The exception is in tzedakah. In this area, one can give and expect that Hashem will make one richer. While one cannot bargain with God and say: "I'll put on tefillin everyday, if You….give me a good livelihood…or I find my soul mate…" and so on, in matters of charity one can make a deal of sorts with God. As the prophet Malachi says that Hashem will "open up the sky for you" should one give one's produce – one can actually test God as it were. What is the reason for this? The reason is simple, but powerful. It is because the universe itself and more specifically, this world, is built on kindness. Charity is the water of life. The only reason God has set up the world that there are some people with much money and some with little and next to nothing is so that the rich should give to the poor. This mimics the very ongoing creative process of God as he extends life to creation continuously infusing it with energy and life.

A small side note: The parsha Re'eh is an acronym for "see" (reish - re'eh) Elul (alef) and heh ("higiah" – is coming). This portion thus heralds the new month of Elul which is a time when Hashem's presence is near in preparation for the high holidays. One should increase in tzedakah.

6) Returning to point 1 on "Anochi". One finds this word used and associated with Moshe, the leader of the generation and the spark of the leader in every generation. This can be found in chapter 11, sentence 21 of Bamidbar, the 4th book of the Torah. Since it is connected with Re'eh – to see – one may infer that in each generation one needs to *see* Moshe, the living embodiment physically of the shepherd that is to lead the flock, the nation of Israel. The

leader, the genius of great stature, is not a politician, rather he has prophetic vision. Like Moshe, he consults and advices; he gives direction. We need to see the leader just as we need air and water and earth and fire – as a kind of basic building block of life. We need the shepherd not simply in spirit, but physically in this world. Then we shall be led out of the desert into the promised land.

7) בנים אתם ליהוה אלהיכם לא תתגדדו ולא תשימו קרחה בין עיניכם למת

"You are children to Hashem, your God – you shall not cut yourselves and you shall not make a bald spot between your eyes for a dead person".

The Ba'al Shem Tov teaches that every Jew is precious to God, just as a child is precious to his parents. You should not forget you are God's child. Therefore, do not harm yourself or defile yourself.

A story is told of a chasid who was going on his way with a wagon. He saw a non-Jew stuck with his wagon in the mud and asked the chasid for help. The chasid replied that he could not to which the non-Jew responded: "You can, you just don't want to". This is a very deep lesson: There are many things we can do and accomplish, but our potential is often short-changed because we believe that we cannot do so. It is not a matter of not being able to, but of the power and strength of will to attempt to do so. Acquiring Torah may seem arduous. If we have the basic desire and will – the "I want to" or "I can" then we surely can do so with God's help.

And this in turn will help the world as a whole – the "non-Jewish" element - so that both he and his wagon shall be freed of the mire. The Messianic Age is an elevation of all peoples of the earth, a vision, a utopia of universal brotherhood, harnessing nature and spiritual light and wisdom.

CHAPTER 5

SHOFTIM

שפטים ושטרים תתן לך בכל שעריך אשר יהוה אלהיך נתן לך לשבטיך ושפטו את העם משפט צדק (1

"Judges and officers shall you appoint in all your cities – which Hashem, your God, gives you – for your tribes; and they shall judge the people with righteous judgement". (16:15)

HaRav Yitzchak Ginsberg notes that there are 7 Shin's in this sentence. This refers to the 7 gates (sha'arecha) and specifically to your gates. This refers to the interface between consciousness and the environment, the senses that take in and give out, so to speak. These are the two ears, the two eyes, the two nostrils and the mouth. Upon each of these "gates" sits a judge (shofet) and when the intellect and senses are engaged in Torah study in order to learn what to do in this world, so one also needs shoterim (officers) in order to apply one's wisdom, to enforce one's understanding. That is, it is not sufficient to simply know the right way, but to, as it were, "force" oneself to apply what I understand, to put in effect the teaching in real life. This is a challenging task. The Rebbe in 1989 writes further that one must put a judge at the gates, that is, the mechanism of input and output, so that one connects with the environment in ways that are in accordance with the Torah and its laws. In this way, a person can ascend in holiness, so that one may perceive God as such from one's very body which is now a fitting receptacle for the Light.

על פי התורה אשר יודוך ועל המשפט אשר יאמרו לך תעשה לא תסור מן הדבר אשר יגידו לך ימין (2 ושמאל

"According to the teaching that they will teach you and according to the judgement that they will say to you, shall you do; you shall not turn from the word that they will tell you, right or left" (17:11).

One is well advised to trust one's own intellect and emotions as some kind of barometer. In every generation there is a shepherd, a Moses of the generation and we have to look for him for he is hidden. This is a Nasi, the leader, a spark of Yaakov and he comes every generation. However, we are enjoined by the Torah that in fact one should listen to the Shepherd or at least one's own Rabbi. One has to do what the Shepherd of the generation decide both for the nation as a whole and in trying to get answers for one's own personal life. This is what assisted in the survival of the Jewish people throughout our exile. If one simply follows one's "own way", one could even come upon what one thinks is true in foreign philosophical and religious systems. For example, both Islam and Christianity are derived from Torah, so one might even stray into false beliefs in following the dictates of one's own "logic".

In fact, Rashi in his commentary, goes so far as to say that even if it seems the Rav is wrong, one has to listen to him. The significance of this is that even though Israel has been scattered to all parts of the world in exile, what kept the connection between brethren who could not connect and communicate, unlike the global village today, was the advice of the Rabbis and sticking to the laws. The Lubavitcher Rebbe goes so far as to say that when a Rav comes and makes a judgement, he changes the reality. Since the Torah is the blueprint of creation, it follows that a dictate of Torah is the essential substrate of reality and reality moves in concord with the law and spirit of Torah. For example, he cites the Rogochover Rebbe who knew the Talmud by heart in perfect detail, who said that a certain tax in Russia should not be according to Torah. Indeed, it was later rescinded. The judgement of the Rav changes reality, that is to say, the Torah is not in heaven but given to man and with it, reality is created, rather than the notion that reality precedes Torah and we do what we can to live in accordance with Torah. It is reversed: One is to follow Torah and then reality too shall follow as it were!

A certain self-nullification (i.e. not having pride) is required in listening and following others, but the Torah makes it clear that one needs to put aside his subjectivity in order to grow and have the willingness to let the Rebbe decide, to give advice, to consult on – a balance between individuality and a sense of acknowledgment of another who is a greater and wiser and therefore one ought to lessen one's ego and be directed by another.

3) שום תשים עליך מלך אשר יבחר יהוה אלהיך בו <u>מקרב</u> אחיך תשים עליך מלך לא תוכל לתת עליך איש נכרי אשר לא אחיך הוא

"You shall surely set over yourself a king whom Hashem, your God, shall choose; from among your brethren shall you set a King over yourself; you cannot place over yourself a foreign man, who is not your brother". (17:15)

Torah tells us that Israel needs a king. Democracy is not necessarily the best form of leadership. It amounts to rule by the mob and politicians that deceive in order to win their favour. But how will we choose a king? The Torah says that God will do so. The kind of king that will be chosen can be derived from the word "mekerev" which is correlated with the word "kiruv" meaning "close". In other words, the king is someone the people can relate to. King David was like a brother to his subjects, the people loved him. As it says in Pirke Avot that the people do what is right when there is a fear of government, where there is law and order, best achieved if the people actually love those who "rule". If this is missing, then there is chaos. We are not to put a non-Jew over us as king– a stranger or foreigner, but rather one of the folk (or even more strongly worded in Torah – one's "brother") of the nation or tribe. In the Gemara (Gitten, p 62) it says that the King Moshiach (Messiah) will be chosen by God when Eliyahu (Elijah) hanavi (the prophet) will return and crown him. It is a great merit from Above.

But what of today when we are bereft of the king? The Gemara says that then it is the "talmudai chachamim", the Rabbis' and the sages that should guide the people – and the Rebbe says that one should search to find a Rabbi (as it says in Malachi 2:7 – "for the lips of the priest ought to preserve knowledge, because he is the messenger of the Lord Almighty nd people seek instruction from his mouth").

4) והיה כשבתו על כסא ממלכתו וכתב לו את משנה התורה הזאת על ספר מלפני הכהנים הלוים

"And it shall be that when he sits on the throne of his kingdom, he shall write for himself two copies of this Torah in a scroll, from before the Kohanim, the Levites" (17:18).

The King is subject to Torah just as any Israelite. The Torah says that he should have two Torah's. One is to be stored in his treasure house and one he is to go out with. The following sentence:

והיתה עמו וקרא בו כל ימיחייו למען ילמד ליראה את יהוה אלהיך לשמר את כל דברי התורה הזאת ואת החקים האלה לעשתם

"It shall be with him and he shall read from it all the days of his life, so that he will learn to fear Hashem, his God, to observe the words of this Torah and these decrees, to perform them" (17:19).

says that he has to read from it all his life. The King, who is the heart of the nation must be deeply connected to the Torah, He thus has to develop fear of G-d and know what it is he has to do. A line further on reads:

לבלתי רום לבבו מאחיו ולבלתי סור מן המצוה ימין ושמאול למען יאריך ימים על <u>ממלכתו</u> הוא ובניו בקרב ישראל

"So that his heart does not become haughty over his brothers and not turn from the commandments right or left, so that he will prolong years over his kingdom, he and his sons amid Israel" (17:20).

This comes to teach us that the king, unlike authoritarian leaders the world over, will not be full of pride and haughtiness in view of his great wealth, property, wives and so on, but rather lead a life of modesty. Long live the king! A source of blessing for others. "Mamlachto " refers to the meaning of "king" as more than simply the persona as leader of a nation, but in our own lives there is a sense that one can be king. Granted on a smaller scale, but no less important. In various domains, such as perhaps in a yeshiva, over oneself, between friends, within one's family unit, in a town and so on – in one or more of these areas, one is like a king. And just as a son may take over kingship, so in one's own family, one wishes for his children to take over the reigns – Long Live the king! – as an inheritance, just as Aaron's sons took over the priesthood.

And we are told here that the king must listen to the prophets (any one of 48 of Israel) and do what it is they require. In this sense, a king is both a great leader and initiator as well as a great follower, subservient to Torah wisdom and awe of that which Created All.

There is a mashal (parable) taught by the Ba'al Shem Tov that a king sent his son to a remote place far from the palace among the ordinary folk. Now it is easier to connect to the king in the palace so that this was a test to see how his son would fair. Does he seek to uplift the place he is now in or is he lowered by its coarseness? After many months, he receives a letter from his father. He is elated and dances with the towns people. The towns people are dancing because they are inebriated by the vodka, while he does so, because he is ecstatic having received a letter from his beloved father. The letter refers to the Torah which is both personal and transcendent.

תמים תהיה עם יהוה אלהיך (5

"You shall be wholehearted with Hashem, your God" (18:13).

The reference here is that we should go with Hashem with simplicity, wholeheartedness and sincerity. Rashi explains this further and writes that one ought to accept whatever comes upon one in life, not caring to delve into what may come about in the future, but simply be open to what God sends one, to make peace with "one's portion".

Shlomo Carlebach, the great Chassid and artist, tells a story of a guy who had a pub, but the pub owner, Jacob was having a hard time earning a living. His wife said that he should go to a big town and find a partner in order to work on the business together and attract more people and so that this partner might also invest in it. This Chassid eventually asked God to be his partner. He promised that half of every rubble he earned would go to Him.

He returned from his trip and told his wife. He felt that all would be good. Indeed, things improved dramatically. And not only did he receive blessing, but because God was his partner he too could give blessings, because Hashem accepted him as a partner.

שלוש ערים תבדיל לך בתוך ארצך אשר יהוה אלהיך נתן לך לרשתה (6

"You shall separate three cities for yourselves in the midst of your land, which Hashem, your God gives you to take possession of it" (19:2)

These cities refer to the cities of refuge. This means that if a person accidently or even purposively kills someone, he can flee to these cities and so escape the wrath and vengeance of the victims' family and friends. The towns were guarded safe-houses until the perpetrator comes to trial.

The Rebbe writes concerning these towns in the spiritual sense. He writes that these special towns or havens refer to the Torah which will keep a person safe even if one should sin, even those done on purpose, God forbid. Just as physically the roads that lead to these cities were wide and easily accessible good roads so that the perpetrator could easily flee to them – and quickly – including "pit stops" along the way, so too the way of Torah and Mitzvot are close to every Jew to take on and perform. It is not remote and Hashem implores one to choose life and then He shall help on one's soul-journey.

Now, to the extent that one chooses life, so the One responds measure for measure. Hashem then gives like the sun, the radiant energy constantly giving, irrespective of the vessel and also like water, the wisdom being channelled to the lowest point just as water flows downward to irrigate the ground. The sun and water remain, whether or not we choose to accept its energy or not. Hashem is there where we call upon Him.

Furthermore, if one should show another person the Way, then Hashem will show you the Way to an even greater extent – measure for measure. Sometimes one's efforts in this regard seem futile and the other person simply does not want Torah wisdom. One can only try, even if it means simply teaching the Alef (the idea of a Creator). One has to be a sign, not one that is mute and inanimate, but full of life and vigour so as to strengthen others, to assist another in coming close to Hashem (adapted from LIkutai Sichot Bet, page 365:1962).

כי יהוה אלהיכם ההלך עמכם להלחם לכם עם איביכם להושיע אתכם (7

"For Hashem, your God, is one that goes with you, to fight for you with your enemies, to save you" (20:4).

Rashi writes concerning this sentence that while the nations claim victory over flesh and blood (by flesh and blood), Israel's victory is that of Hashem. All Israel's success is from the power of Hashem and it is He that has allowed Israel to prevail even as the great armies and empires have arisen and fallen – the Persians, the Assyrians, the Babylonians, the Philistines, the Greeks, the Romans, Christianity and modern nations states, including the rise of Islam and so on. Somehow, a tiny nation in a small piece of land has survived having injected its ideas of the sanctity of life; of the One God; of the God immanent in history; of the Holy Book and the Holy Land throughout the worlds in its 3000 year pus history. We too must go out in the world and be fitting vessels of His light. This winning can only be with our effort. Still we yearn for ultimate peace and the ultimate victory – netzach – of God with the restoration of the Temple and the infusing of holy light from Jerusalem and thence throughout the whole world.

CHAPTER 6

Ki Seitze

כי תצא למלחמה <u>על</u> איביך ונתנו יהוה אלהיך בידך ושבית שביו (1

"When you will go out to war against your enemies, and Hashem, your God, will deliver him into your hands, and you will capture its (people as), captives" (21:10).

The word used, namely "על" refers to the idea that in combat one is "above" one's enemies. The Torah is referring both to physical and spiritual enemies. In the realm of spirit, one must be above one's animal soul and evil inclination so as to overcome the pull of the body and the cravings and lustful desires. Similarly, in physical battle, one must not succumb to the tricks of the enemy. And so spiritually, one has to use his very arguments to teach the opposite. He may say that there is evil in the world and therefore an absence of a loving God. One can turn the argument around and say the presence of darkness is precisely the reason why God put man here, that is to combat it and bring God into the world so to speak; to act as God's partner in the overpowering of darkness with the light of Torah.

2) Referring to the first sentence of the parsha as above, one can discern another level. The sentence is saying that when a person "goes out" from his connection with God, then one enters a battlefield, the exigencies, and vicissitudes of life. This world is the world of separation where a glimmer of God is hardly distinct. Armed with Torah, divine wisdom, one can fulfil one's purpose, which is to unite and bring together that which is separate into a holy unity reflecting the eternity and oneness of God. This is shalom or peace. The book of Tanya explains that this is the lowest of innumerable worlds that God has created and continues to create every moment and unless one has the tools to transform it, namely Torah and Mitzvot, one is forever caught in a battle and will feel the broken separation of this plane or dimension of existence.

The next sentence of Torah reads:

וראית בשביה אשת יפת תאר וחשקת בה ולקחת לך לאשה

"and you will see among its captivity a woman who is beautiful of form, and you will desire her, you will take her to yourself for a wife" (21:11).

This sentence refers to the idea that though the Torah understands human desire especially during the terrible reality of war, the soldier has an option to act on his desires but not without a specific following of certain procedures and laws. For the physical beauty of a woman is as a result of the breaking of the vessels, that cataclysmic residue of the initial array of sefirot. Her true beauty, however is her spiritual aspect.

The problem is that when the eyes focus on something in the world and is attracted by it, so the heart desires it. The Torah is saying that should such desires arise, there is an option, but one (the soldier) would have to abide by Torah law in order to be with her – and in the midst of battle (a far cry from the armies of the nations throughout the bloody reality of human history). The primary lesson here is that one has to take one's physical desires and sacrifice it towards a higher purpose, for the sake of holiness and to connect with the higher worlds. If one is merely a slave to one's desires, the physical cannot be elevated and is in exile, unable to reveal the holy sparks lodged therein.

3) The first sentence is particularly powerful, so let's draw a further idea from it considering the volumes of commentary expounded on it. The Rebbe, drawing from the Zohar explains that the time of prayer is a time of war. Who is the enemy? The power, the will that desires and the power of prayer is to calm it down, to avert oneself from attachment and encumbrance in the physical, material world. With this as a basis, one then graduates to a level where there is space and feeling for the love of God. Thus, the Rebbe writes in the Ma'amar that one's work in prayer is to transform and change the pleasures one is ordinarily attracted to and reach for more spiritual ends.

The Ma'amar continues and explains that there is nothing that is ultimately bad that occurs in this world for in truth everything emanates from the higher world so that everything in its source is good. In fact, since everything is truly from Hashem, the yetzer hara (the evil inclination) has a good purpose, that is, through prayer we struggle with "him", we get close to the animal soul and connect it with her source. And everyday the yetzer hara with all its desires renews itself, finds all sorts of insidious arguments to stake its claim (on the body) and so that is why one must wake up resolute for battle in order to coax it and toward the spiritual, responding creatively and intelligently each time to its renewed strategy, for it is the nature of reality that its constantly changes every minute.

Man is given an allotted time on earth. These years are not given to the Godly soul which does not need a tikkun (fixing) for she is perfect. Thus, the mission is for the Godly soul to elevate the animal soul, to gather sparks lost in shivrat hakeilim (the shattering of the vessels). Thus, in this world, which is likened to a deep pit, one must raise up these sparks or embers of the cataclysmic creation, and Hashem has calculated the time needed for each soul to elevate the sparks that belong to her and fulfil one's mission.

The Rebbe thus argues that one must work through prayer through understanding the words of prayer and cleaving to God not simply requesting that our needs be fulfilled (although that is part of prayer), but the spiritual work of connecting to the Creator. At some point, one might reach a junction. Here one can choose the way of prayer or the way of Torah. That is, one can choose prayer which is defined as a kind of war or studying Torah, which is the way of peace (see further Proverbs 3:17). Although the mitzvah of prayer is a basic obligation and to be chosen over other mitzvah's in general, it is the way of Torah that is so powerful, for here the evil inclination and the animal soul hold little sway.

4) With reference to the opening sentence once again, let's see what further can be learned. When you go out to war refers to when the soul comes out or descends from the higher worlds. In some way the footsteps, the path of a person is predestined, kind of like fate, planned by God. That is, a particular portion of the world is given to that soul to rectify and sort out and that part of the world, is, as it were, waiting for that soul to redeem it, a task given before one is even born (one is usually not aware of such a task, however).

The Rebbe elicits four dimensions of personhood referred to by four different names/concepts/titles – to achieve such a destiny and destiny – and this provides a map of that which needs to be refined, namely the body/animal soul/environment.

1) There is "Adam" – this refers to a high level achieved in a person's mind/brain and knowledge. There is 2) "Ish" - this refers to a high level of refinement in feelings/the heart; then 3) "Gever" – one who is aware of weakness and is trying to develop what's missing; one who tries to overcome something and struggles to solve problems and to make efforts in Torah. 4) "Enosh" – someone who has weakness in brain/heart. Here one is thus called upon

to make the best of one's character traits as they are defined as the elements of creation – earth, air, water and fire – as elucidated in the Tanya. The negative aspect of these elements: earth is sloth and melancholy; air is frivolity and triviality and gossip; water are the various physical pleasures of the world and fire is anger, pride and arrogance and "gever" tries to surmount them.

5) לא תראה את שור אחיך או את שיו נדחים והתעלמת מהם השב תשיבם לאחיך

"You shall not see the ox of your brother or his lamb/kid cast off; you shall surely return

them to your brother" (22:1).

This verse refers to the idea that one should not "hide" from the difficulties and pain of another when the other person feels lost and rejected and disconnected. One has to help the other person and do what one can in order to alleviate his suffering and loss and aid him in finding that which he lost. On a spiritual level, it is as if he lost that which is truly his, namely his spiritual connection to God and the Jewish people and feels rejected. One must return what Is essentially his. There are times when one can ignore the loss of another, for example there is a halachah that an old man who finds something is not obligated to return it if the lost item is too heavy, and so there is a sense in which some situations are simply not one's business such as in a case when that other person does not want to be helped or wants no part in the spirituality of the Torah, for example. There are times when the other person is not ready to hear words of Torah and scoffs at it; he may even hate you for trying to intervene. In such a case it is best to say nothing. Sometimes one has to let go.

However, the usual case is that one can assist. The following line reads:

ואם לא קרוב אחיך אליך ולא ידעתו ואספתו אל תוך ביתך והיה עמך עד דרש אחיך אתו והשבתו לו

"If your brother is not near you and you do not know him, then you shall bring it inside your house, and it shall remain with you until your brother's inquiring about it, then you shall return it to him" (22:2).

Even if one cannot find the one who lost an object, one must try to find him and not give up on the quest. One should not simply avoid or evade the situation. Even if it is someone one hardly knows, one must try to return it to him, however far he may be. This then refers to the mesirus nefesh (the sacrifice of one's soul) in going out of one's way for one's brother, a true act of loving one's fellow. Todays with social media, a kind Torah word can go far and recover the "lost" gems of Israel that one may not even be aware of and thus return to him his spiritual essence that has been floundering in the desert for so very long. As the Ba'al Shem Tov says, one has to give one's time, energy and wealth to love a fellow, even one has never even met – this is true mesirus nefesh!

6) Parshas Ki Teitzei is always read during the month of Elul. We read the Tehillim (Psalm 27) during this time everyday in the morning (shachris) and afternoon (mincha) prayers. The Rebbe shares with us some ideas around King David's plea:

It begins with a reference to "my light". This refers to a request to God that He should direct and lead one with His wisdom; that one should see the good way to follow and to know what is the right path to follow.

Yet it is not sufficient to simply know what to do. One has to have the power to implement these ideas in a world where one is tested and there are many barriers to spiritual service and a life of holiness. This is the reference to the word "vayishi" ("my salvation") that follows "light" (ori – my light) and we recognise we need God's help to overcome the animal soul and the evil inclination.

So, a third concept assures us that we can be successful. "Maoz Chaya" – Hashem is the strength of one's life. That with light and His salvation comes the strength to not only be victorious here and there but to complete the job, to rise from good to better, to go from strength to strength and from stage to stage in divine service and crucially in preparation for Rosh Hashanah which is to bring a new year, a new man and a new light.

7) כי תבנה בית חדש ועשית מעקה לגגך ולא תשים דמים בביתך כי יפל הנפל ממנו

"If you build a new house, you shall make a fence for your roof, so that you will not place blood in your house if one who falls shall fall from it" (22:8).

This line refers to a fence that needs to be erected on the roof or balcony so that there should not be an accident. There is a special blessing one even says over it. The Rebbe explains that this law hints at the idea that when one "builds a new house", that is to say, takes on a new challenge, there are inevitably battles and barriers that surface and in such a case, one has to build a fence so that one does not fall as one takes on this new challenge. For example, there is a vast difference between yeshivah life or school and then entering into a new phase of engagement with the world. The answer is that just as the fence is higher than the house, so in dealing with new situations one has to create a Torah stronghold and bless Hashem who has commanded one so that one's movement from one set of circumstances to another shall be a smooth transition and defined and blessed by God. In this way one can effect the world through Torah, connecting with the unity of God even when it appears that one is further from holiness. In so doing, one reveals the presence of God within limited dimensions.

CHAPTER 7

KI SAVO

והיה <u>כי</u> תבוא אל הארץ אשר יהוה אלהיך נתן לך נחלה וירשתה וישבת בה (1

"It will be when you enter the land that Hashem, your God, gives you as an inheritance, and you take possession of it, and dwell in it" (26:1).

The Ba'al HaTurim (Yaakov ben Asher, a famous, 11th Century commentator) explains that the "ki" of the first word of the parsha's name has the gematria 30 referring to the 30 righteous (tzaddikim) in the world at a given time. Added to the 6 letters that comprise the words "ki tavo" we have a total of 36. This refers to the 36 righteous individuals in each generation and who are the foundation of the world.

Sometimes we know who these individuals are, but usually they are hidden. The Ba'al Shem Tov, for example hid himself for ten years between the ages of 26 to 36 and on the 18th Elul (in the year 1734) he revealed himself having received a message on high that he should spread the wellsprings of Torah and Chassidut.

והיה כי תבוא אל הארץ אשר יהוה אלהיך נתן לך נחלה וירשתה וישבת בה (2

"It will be when you enter the land that Hashem, your God, gives you as an inheritance, and you take possession of it, and dwell in it" (26:1).

And when we go into the land, Hashem gives us this mitzvah as revealed in the following line:

ולקחת מראשית כל פרי האדמה אשר תביא מארצך אשר יהוה אלהיך נתן לך ושמת בטנא והלכת אל המקום אשר יבחר יהוה אלהיך לשכן שמו שם

"that you shall take the first of every fruit of the ground that you bring in from your land that Hashem, your God, gives you, and you shall put it in a basket and go to the place that Hashem, your God, will choose, to make His Name rest there" (26:2).

Once the Jewish People have conquered the Land of Israel, they are to observe the mitzvah of first fruits, namely "bikkurim". These refer to the fruits of the seven species which are to be taken and put in a basket and taken to the Temple to be given to the kohan (priest).

Now the Torah has both a body (the basket) and a soul (the fruits). The body are the "halachot", the bottom-line laws and rules to be followed and done. The soul refers to its inner meaning, the spiritual dimension. The Rebbe Rashab (5th Rebbe) explains that the first sentence above using the word for land (ha'aretz) has another meaning. It is connected with the word "want" (rotzeh); it shares the same root letters. This implies that when one has reached the level of wanting to do what Hashem wants, which is true conquering of the land (of the body), so one has to know that this is indeed one's mission, the shlichus (mission) and a gift from Above, an inheritance (as it says in this first line). It runs deep for such an inheritance is built into one's mind/soul/DNA, just as an animal is said to possess instinct.

The first line says "vayashavta" (and you shall dwell) which is to say that this "will" as explained above is like light or water and it needs a vessel so that one's drive to serve Hashem ought to be practical and fit within this world as such. How is this achieved?

When it says that we are to go to the place ("halachata...") that Hashem will choose, we are to understand that it is not we or I that run and organise the world, that in fact a single life is so infinitely small compared to the great expanse of the cosmos and its infinite details, and Hashem himself has given Israel a mission which is precisely to publicize the name of God in the world and in particular, wherever one (happens to) find oneself.

The method for doing so was already mapped out by the patriarch Abraham[4]. The important point is that one assists others to acknowledge Hashem, the King of the world rather than all

---

[4] Abraham comes from the root "haivri", that is the "othersider", one who opposed to all other philosophies and ideas of the time in his belief in an invisible God, monotheism, as opposed to the paganism of his time. His method for helping others along this path of discovery was to put his tent in a strategic place in the desert so that people would come across it on their way. He would offer them food and drink to ease their journey and when they wanted to pay him for his kindness, he refused to take money and simply said that they are to bless the One God from whence the sustenance is derived.

the nonsense under the sun. Even if one does the minimum -say a blessing and one tehillim (psalm) a day that is still effective. Ideally, one should seek out another Jew as the Rebbe taught and give the best one can with mesirus nefesh (sacrifice of the soul). One has to use all one's gifts. If one can refine diamonds then that is what one must to do – Hashem wants us to live up to our potential. The only question Is whether one is using one's gift to spread the Divine wisdom or not, but certainly one must "give of our first fruits" in order to serve God in joy, in order to help others realise their Godly source and in order to be a creative partner with Hashem and dispel the darkness with light.

3) Please have a look at the following lines in Devarim:- 26:6-11.

וירעו אתנו המצרים ויענונו ויתנו עלינו עבדה קשה

"The Egyptians mistreated us and afficted us, and placed hard work upon us" (26:6).

ונצעק אל יהוה אלהי אבתינו וישמע יהוה את קלנו וירא את ענינו ואת עמלנו ואת לחצנו

"Then we cried out to Hashem, the God of our forefathers, and Hashem heard our voice and saw our affliction, our travail, and our oppression" (26:7).

 In these lines, one can note a conceptual pattern if one picks out a single word in each line. In 6 - וירעו – refers to the hard Egyptian slavery where not only was it bad, but rather the Egyptians influenced the Children of Israel to themselves also be bad. It is the exile itself that causes the waters of Egypt to influence Israel negatively.

In 7 – ענינו – refers to how the Jewish people were tortured and made poor.

In 8 – ויצאנו – Hashem hears our cry and comes to save us.

In 9 – ויבאנו – and Hashem brings us to the Place; he frees us.

In 10 - ארץ זבת חלב ודבש – He brings us to a beautiful land. The last three letters of the description of this land - ארץ זבת חל**ב** וד**בש**

spell Shabbat (shin, bet, tuf) so that entry into this land is holier and on a higher level than any other place on earth, charged as it is with a special light and providence.

And 11 – ושמחת – and one has to be happy and joyous with all the good that Hashem has done, to be grateful for what He gives and even though things might be better – and so we pray – there are in fact many positive things. So here is an evolution from slavery to freedom, from being without a home to finding a home and from a painful existence to one inspired by God Himself.

את יהוה האמרת היום להיות לך לאלהים וללכת בדרכיו ולשמר חקיו ומצותיו ומשפטיו ולשמע בקלו (4

"You have distinguished Hashem today to be a God for you, and to walk in His ways, and to observe His statutes, His commandments, and His laws, and to listen to His voice" (26:17).

"He'emarti" in this sentence refers to choosing/distinguishing/emphasizing among several alternatives. Among the infinite details in the universe, one sees the unity and oneness of God and puts this idea of God above all other subjects, recognising that it is this that infuses all variation with its energy. This word is also used (as in the name Amir – same root letters) and its meaning is that of the highest branch of the tree, alluding to the idea that the subject and mystery of God is higher than all other branches of knowledge.

The very next line reads:

"ויהוה האמירך היום להיות לו לעם סגלה כאשר דבר לך ולשמר כל מצותיו"

"And Hashem has distinguished you today to be for Him a treasured people, as He spoke to you, and to observe all His commandments" (26:18).

Here this sentence mirrors the preceding one. Just as we choose and distinguish Hashem among all avenues of knowledge and wisdom, so He distinguishes/chooses the Children of Israel to be a treasured nation among many nations.

The Rebbe likens the idea of treasure to a king who has many gems, gold and silver and diamonds and so on. Some of these precious stone adorn the crown; some might be used as gifts to nobles of other lands or to pay his own ministers, yet there are some that have no function. These treasures are simply there for their own sake and the Rebbe likens this to a Jew, who even without the Torah and Mitzvot, simply by virtue of his being and essence – a Godly soul attached to a body – is itself a treasure, irrespective of what he does. Such is the preciousness of the soul and such is the unbounded love of Hashem for his creations. Of courseת He wants us to behave and do the right thing, but ultimately it is a matter of unconditional love like a parent for his/her child.

5) In 28:1-6 (by all means, have a look therein), we find the details of blessing that will occur should one follow in Hashem's ways. He promises that Israel will be "supreme" among the nations of the earth; that one will be blessed in the city and in the field; that blessings of children will come, as with livelihood and finally that one will be blessed in your coming and your going and iterates these points in the next few lines. Rashi explains regarding the last blessing mentioned that this refers to the idea that one's going out and coming is a reference to death and to coming into being, being born and that just as one is free of sin upon entering the world, so one will leave the world pure.

6) "וראו כל עמי הארץ כי שם יהוה נקרא עליך ויראו ממך"

"Then all the peoples of the earth will see that the Name of Hashem is proclaimed over you, and they will revere you" (28:10).

That the name of Hashem is upon Israel explained by Rashi as a reference to the "teffilin", specifically the head "tefillin". It has a connection to the gimel and dalet, 3 and 4 respectively, namely the letter "shin's" on the head "teffilin", one of which has three "legs" and another four. This hints at gomel (3) dalet (4) – to give to the poor. The very construction of the gimmel is a man running, while the dalet is like a man running away. So, the gimmel pursues the dalet, indicating that the work is that a person should try to run to influence another positively, offering guidance and support.

The gimmel also refers to the three higher worlds – "atzilut", "beriah" and "yetzirah", while dalet (the quintessential 4 directions) refers to this world, the realm of "asiyah". The good that is received on this plane is as a result of these higher dimensions is the channelling of 7 (combination of 3 and 4) and these allude to the menorah of the Temple whose light is not simply physical, but spiritual as it lights up the whole world giving fear to one's enemies/the darkness – just as "tefillin" does – and creating a better world in the process.

7) If one reads chapter 28, lines 15-49, one will find 98 curses and sicknesses should Israel not heed the words of Torah. The Rebbe notes that we read of such curse in all its terrible detail just before both "Rosh HaShanah" and "Shavuot". The reason for this is that going through these harsh forms of punishment is really a spiritual cleansing so that we should have a fitting vessel for all the good that these holidays will bring. For in truth there is nothing bad that comes from the higher worlds.

Such a perception is part of the spiritual make-up of the sages. Two stories are told in this regard reputed to be 2000 years old or so. The saying of Rabbi Nachum Ish Gamzu that "this too is for the good" and Rabbi Akiba, who wrote in Aramaic a slightly different version – "Everything Hashem does is for the good". The former wrote when the second temple still stood while in Rabbi Akiba's time, it was destroyed. Two stories explain the slight differential nuance.

It is told that Rabbi Akiba went on a journey. He took a donkey, a chicken and a candle. The donkey was so that his body would not disturb him and the animal could help with the load and the task of carrying; the chicken was used so as to wake him up in the morning and the candle so that he could study Torah at night. He came to a certain town and asked if he could stay there so that he would not have to face the danger of the forest. They said that they do not accept guests. And so he was left for the dark, dangerous wilderness.

At night, a lion came and ate his donkey; a cat ate his chicken and the wind extinguished his flame. He was bewildered and did not understand why all this happened, only to learn that at night some bandits came and took the townsfolk as slaves. So now the sage understood that Hashem had protected him and the death of the chicken and donkey and the light of the candle were necessary for else the bandits would have found him and taken him into captivity as well.

In the case of Ish Gamzu – he was on a mission on behalf of Israel to give a present to the Emperor of Rome in order to placate him, namely a box of beautiful diamonds and pearls. Along the way, he stayed at an Inn. That night he was robbed of the precious jewels. Instead of the precious materials, he was left with a box of sand. He immediately said to himself that this too is for the good and some good will come of it. When he showed the sand box to the leader of Rome, he was livid. Yet just that night Eliyahu ha Navi (Elijah, the prophet) had come to the Caesar and told him that the sand had miraculous powers to win wars and gain victory. The Caesar tested this strange offering and was victorious in battle. The result was that the decree against Israel by Rome was rescinded.

The Ba'al Shem Tov teaches based on these stories where apparent negativity is in fact very positive, for Hashem's providence is for the good – and certainly the ultimate good. In parshas Noach (Bereishis – Genesis), the word used for window is "tzohar", a word that also refers to "troubles". It is also connected to the word "ratza", run. The teaching is that one should always be in motion, turning troubles into light, just as a window is the liminal point between inside and outside, drawing in the light, space, air, and just as Noah sent the pigeon to find land, so adversity has hidden light and is the very mechanism for healing and success. This is a training of course, since sometimes it is difficult to see the good as it is covered over in this, the lowest of all worlds.

CHAPTER 8

Nitzavim/Vayeilech

1) The first line of Nitzavim reads:

אתם נצבים היום כלכם לפני יהוה אלהיכם ראשיכם שבטיכם זקניכם ושטריכם כל איש ישראל

"You are standing today, all of you, before Hashem, your God: Your heads, your elders, and your officers – all the men of Israel" (29:9).

This line reflects the unity of the Jewish people who are a single soul/body connecting each of us since we all share a spark of God. The next line טפכם נשיכם וגרך אשר בקרב מחניך מחטב עציך עד שאב מימיך which translates as "your small children, your woman, and your convert who is in the midst of your camp, from the hewer of wood to the drawer of water" (29:10). goes into greater detail regarding the different parts of the Jewish people, referring to "Eitsecha" (hewer of wood) and "meimecha" (drawer of water). These occupations help the people in general to survive and thrive. Even the more physical and less intellectual kinds are work are just as significant, just as all parts of the body matter – regardless of the level of Jew, all matter as part of this organic unity.

Chassidut explains the deeper layer of meaning. Water refers to all kinds of pleasures and desires (drawer of water). The teaching here is to get closer to Hashem,. one has to reduce the desire and expression of such lusts. Judaism is not opposed to pleasure as such and is not an ascetic religion, but one has to temper and moderate such proclivities to make it conducive to sensitivity for more spiritual matters. This process of redirecting and transforming such energies is known in Chassidut as "etkafiyah" ("to coerce" or "force" in order to quell desires). The Rambam himself argues that the best and most temperate way is to seek the "middle way" (Mishneh Torah).

Cutting trees refers to the work of not dealing with certain thoughts, that is, to prune and create proper form or spiritual beauty by controlling or even banishing certain thoughts that pop into mind; it is the ability to not deal with certain negative or dangerous thoughts, and to thus be of pure mind. As the Ba'al Shem Tov says – one is where one's thoughts are – and thus the quality and intensity of one's inner world is of paramount importance. It is vital for both physical and spiritual health or state of being.

2) Nitzavim and Vayeilech are considered as one parsha and in fact we often read them together on a given shabbas before Rosh Hashanah and during the month of Elul. One can extract from these two names of the parshas the word "Melech" – king (the last letter of nitzavim and the last and penultimate letters of vayelech). The remaining letters – nun; tzadi; bet; yud (x2) and vav – total 168. 168 is 24 x 7. Putting these sequences together, the following idea emerges: In order to be a king over oneself one has to try become closer to God during all one's hours each week (24/7).

What is a king? The "mem" refers to "moach" (brain or mind); the "lamed" to "lev" or heart and the "cuf" refers to "caved" or liver. This is the correct order for a king: First one has to activate the mind which in turn produces feelings and finally moves to action, the liver whose function it is to clean and filter the blood, the action-orientated aspect of a person. When the letters that comprise "Melech" (king) are not in this sequence, then one is a "lamech" and a "chelem", that is, like a fool or clown. By endeavouring to be like a king, one creates order out of chaos and since each person is defined as a world, one can have kingship over one's world and rule, so to speak, in the best way possible.

3) The Rambam writes that Israel's elders, prophets and the wise desire the days of the Messiah. Such days will be characterised by the fact that Israel will no longer be pursued by the nations and will be given rest from impending violence. Today we have to protect our borders. However, even today we are perhaps seeing the arrival of the Messiah. Many of Israel's enemies no longer pose a threat or are themselves collapsing and some even want peace with Israel. The point of all this is that Israel should be left alone to deal with the Torah, in peace and safety.

The days of the Messiah will be a time when the knowledge of God is spread throughout the world. In a kind of vision as espoused by Rav Kook, as the secular sciences and arts will be seen as expressions of the divine. Such knowledge will be used to understand the mind of God as it were and co-join with a deeper understanding of Torah. In these days, "one's heart of stone" will be transformed into "a heart of flesh" (Yeheschial 36:25). This means that the coarseness toward spiritual matters will be removed and a truly human, humane and empathetic heart will be in its place. It may *seem* that humanity is far from this goal today. Perhaps it is simply the darkness before the dawn and the change is coming.

The King Messiah, a descendent of King David and almost as great as the prophet Moses will bring the diaspora back to Israel and will bring the nations to worship the One, true, invisible God. Many things shall remain the same in the new world: work; property and land ownership and farming and so on – only the Messiah will create a situation of greater spiritual awareness and also towards fulfilling Mitzvot that today we cannot, such as the Mitzvot surrounding the holy Temple.

4) הנסתרת ליהוה אלהינו ונגלת לנו ולבנינו עד עולם לעשות את כל דברי התורה הזאת

"The hidden things are for Hashem, our God, but the revealed things are for us and our children forever, to carry out all the words of the Torah" (29:28).

The hidden things only Hashem knows. We can but see what is revealed. One does not have to be a prophet to see what another does externally, say giving charity or wearing tzitzit and so on – but the hidden, that which is within a person, only Hashem truly knows. It is the private world within – one's thoughts, one's love and awe and so on that only Hashem knows and can account for.

The idea is a kind of "love-sickness" for God. The paradigm example is a love a man may have for a woman. It can a be a kind of "drug" colouring whatever happens to him in a given day, forever seeing her in all that happens and dwelling on her in his mind and heart. This, according to Rambam is the kind of parallel energy and even more so, that one should feel for God. But how can one love that which is essentially a spiritual reality? The "shema"[5] tells one to love God with "all one's heart" and one's possessions, one's very being and fibre. But how might this be achieved with a purely spiritual, unfathomable "entity"? One has to cultivate this sensitivity and the alluring words of the Song of Songs hints at such a bond.

In fact, one might think of all one's relationships and especially the powerful drive between a man and woman as an instance of a gift that Hashem Himself might bestow on one and in fact, such a thought process would apply to all loving relationships – they are all expressions

---

[5] The Shema is a meditation that we are to utter twice a day to understand and be one with the understanding that there is ultimately only the One God in all the worlds.

of the ultimate bond that is between oneself and the Creator. The point is that the "lovesickness" brings a certain holiness and willingness to do whatever the other wishes; it may even lead to odd decisions – a kind of holy spirit for the good.

ושבת עד יהוה אלהיך ושמעת בקלו ככל אשר אנכי מצוך היום אתה ובניך בכל לבבך ובכל נפשך (5

"And you will return unto Hashem, your God, and listen to His voice, according to everything that I command you today, you and your children, with all your heart and all your soul" (30:2).

"Adonai" is a very sublime and high level or name of God, whereas "Elohim" refers to God's power in nature/limitation and from which human power is derived. If one follows in Hashem's ways as enjoined in this line, then He answers as in 30:3, where it says in the Torah that God will have mercy on us, gather-in the scattered exiles and grant us freedom in the Land of Israel. Furthermore, in 30:6, it recounts how Hashem will "circumcise our hearts" and where it says את לבבך ואת לבב ("your heart and the heart…"), one will notice that the initial letters of each word in this phrase spell "Elul" hinting at the congruence of these two parshiyot that are always read in Elul preceding Rosh Hashanah.

כי המצוה הזאת אשר אנכי מצוך היום לא נפלאת הוא ממך ולא רחקה הוא...לא בשמים הוא לאמר (6 מי יעלה לנו השמימה ויקחה לנו וישמענו אתה ונעשנה

"For the commandment that I command you today, it is not hidden from you and it is not distant" (30:11)…"It is not in the heavens, for you to say: who can ascend to the heavens for us and take it for us; and let us hear it, so that we can perform it" (30:12).

The phrase that reads – "who shall ascend to the heavens" – is such that the first letter of each of these words – mem, yud, lamed and heh spell "milah" – circumcision, as noted in a famous maamar of the Rebbe (chassidut, Likutei Torah). This implies that the Torah is already imprinted on our very body as a covenant that cannot be torn asunder; it is part of our being and not something that is too far out of reach either physically or spiritually. The point is – as Rashi also elucidates – that the Torah can be studied, assimilated and embodied here on earth and one need not soar into the heavens to find it. On the other hand, what is alluded to is that enacting Torah here on earth is a ladder that leads "above". Torah is meant to be lived here on earth and is not something so concealed as to remain a secret, a closed book. If only one should search after it as if it were a treasure, securing "wealth" both in this world and the next.

כי קרוב אליך הדבר מאד בפיך ולבבך לעשתו (7

"Rather the matter is very near to you, in your mouth and in your heart, to perform it" (30:14).

This sentence is the beginning and very foundation of the classic Chabad text, the Tanya, by the founder of Chabad chassidut, namely the first Rebbe, Rav Shneur Zalman of Liadi.

The principle underlying this sentence and the basis for the Tanya, is that observing the Torah is "in one's heart", that is, one's thought. It is in one's "mouth", that is speech and it is in what one does – "performs", that is, actions. Thus, the Torah requires the inclusion of all three garments of the soul, namely thought, speech and action. To the extent that one can do this, so one's Godly soul is given full expression within one's very body and one may ascend in holiness and cleave to the Source of All. It is not sufficient to simply meditate. It is not sufficient to speak of Torah and not apply it. And it is not sufficient to mechanically observe the commandments without intention, thought and the movement of the lips in say prayer or study. And although this may seem a difficult and even burdensome task, Hashem tells us in the Torah that in fact it is very close to one to actualise this.

The world may appear dark at times. It may be difficult to be disciplined and follow the structure of a Torah life. Yet Hashem says that in fact, this is achievable and that this can be done within this world, thus producing light in the world and expression of the soul. It is this that produces joy, for squandered potential is painful and sad while its full and creative expression brings happiness.

It is this connection to the Torah that may be encapsulated and summarised by the following line in "Vayeilech":

ועתה כתבו לכם את השירה הזאת ולמדה את בני ישראל שימה בפיהם למען תהיה לי השירה הזאת לעד בבני ישראל

"So now, write this song for yourselves, and teach it to the Children of Israel, place it in their mouth, so that this song shall be for Me a witness against the Children of Israel" (31:19).

From this line, it was extrapolated that every Jew has a Mitzvah to write for himself a sefer Torah. The Rebbe explain that this could translate that a letter in Torah or even a Torah book might be ascribed or sponsored by someone or in dedication. It also means that a home should have Torah books and that one supports Torah learning. In order for the Torah to be, in truth – close - as one read in the preceding parsha is now given full weight by saying that one should fill one's mind and home with ideas related to Torah, that is with books of Torah. It is thus through intellectual understanding that Torah comes close to a person, for what one thinks about effects the outcome of feeling and thence one's actual behaviour.

CHAPTER 9

HA'AZINU

האזינו השמים ואדברה ותשמע הארץ אמרי פי (1

"Give ear, O Heavens, and I will speak; and may the earth hear the words of my mouth" (32:1).

Here, Moses is speaking to the world. He asks the sky and earth to listen. The first reference ("ha'azinu") refers to speaking to someone you are close to, while the other expression of hearing ("tishmah") refers to speaking to one that is more distant. These two expressions of hearing sound in subtly similar ways is found only one other time in the Torah in Isaiah (1:2), though in the opposite way, where the prophet says that the sky should hear ("tishmah") and the earth too ("ha'azinu"). Why are the expressions reversed in this case?

In the first instance, Moses is speaking. Moshe Rebeinu (Moses our teacher) equals 613 in gematria, the total number of "mitzvot". Moses was thus close to the sky, a receptacle of the law and therefore far from the earth, that which is simply a tool for the "mitzvot". For Isaiah, the mode of service is reversed – the material things are the basis for a spiritual life. The Rebbe writes that this explains two modes of service: "shamayim" or sky refers to Torah study while "earth" ("eretz") refers to all modes of secular work and interest.

Now, we should not simply be of the sky or the earth, but a combination and all Jews inter-include one another, so that Torah scholars should have some work and working people should have some Torah (study). Judaism is not simply a philosophy or an academic study, but rather one should learn in order to do and thence grow and transform. The things of the world should be used or shunned in accordance with the commandments. We should have the will – I want to build a palace (God's home on earth) - and we simply ask for the tools and materials to do so, rather than simply materiality as an end in itself.

בהנחל עליון גיום בהפרידו בני אדם יצב גבלת עמים למספר בני ישראל (2

"When the supreme One gave nations their portion, when he separated the children of man, He set the borders of peoples according to the number of the Children of Israel" (32:8).

This is quite a concentrated and condensed sentence. Rashi explains four different aspects of this sentence as it unfolds:

a) he gave every nation a piece of land

b) each such nation has different tribes/peoples/cultures within a single land.

c) there are borders between these countries/nations

d) that the 70 nations and the 70 languages parallel the number of the Children of Israel, namely, the 70 souls that descended into Egypt, so that the whole narrative of human history and the Jews as a microcosm of such events, is planned.

אדם יצב גבלת – has a particular meaning to the author of this book. The gimmel and yud spell the authors surname – Guy – while the word יצב re-arranged spell Tzvi, the authors father's name. Each of us can find his name in the Torah especially in this parsha in either a hidden or revealed way.

There is a sense that each Jew has a spark of Moshiach and the nation as a whole are witnesses to Hashem and the general soul and connection to all the peoples of the earth, for the revelation of the Messiah is an upliftment of all peoples to a higher consciousness.

3) כי חלק יהוה עמו יעקב חבל נחלתו

"For Hashem's share is His people; Jacob, the portion of His possession" (32:9).

This verse basically explains that His portion or part, is the fact that every Jew has a part of God within, that is, a Godly soul. This is an inheritance of the patriarchs, the righteous Abraham, Isaac and Jacob as they built and mapped out the path for the future nation.

The Godly soul itself is perfect. She needs no "tikkun" or fixing. Her job is to repair the animal soul, the body, the brain, the feelings, actions and so on as well as his part/place ("chelek") in the world and in the process improve the world somewhat. One has to seek God each day and do the right action so as to benefit our surroundings. As the Ba'al Shem Tov explains, "zahir" means not only to be careful and scrupulous about what one does whether a small or a great task, but also to give "light", that is to give a great shine to what one is involved with in this world and to dispel the darkness of anger, hate, judgement and so on. Ultimately, God wants a persons' heart, the deepest and most sincere point within. This is a basis for a real and mature relationship.

כנשר יעיר קנו על גוזליו ירחף יפרש כנפיו יקחהו ישאהו על אברתו (4

"Like an eagle arousing his nest hovering over his young, he spreads his wings, he takes it, he carries it on his pinions" (32:11).

The "peshat" (literal interpretation) is itself profound. When an eagle comes to its nest, it does not do so immediately and in one swoop. It motions with its wings and he carefully goes about waking its young. It is such that the eagle is said to touch and not to touch, to simply glide and hover over. This metaphor is like the end of days. God will not startle or scare the peoples of the earth. Instead, He will slowly draw out the process of redemption, allowing a long process to manifest his presence – the conscious awareness of people that indeed the "eagle" is here and ready to give to His children. The change – the massive changes of the Messianic redemption – will happen gradually so that the vessel can receive it safely. A New Age will dawn just as the sun slowly rises as it were.

And just as the eagles' wings protect his children from arrows, so Hashem will look after us just as at the redemption from Egyptian slavery. The eagle protects its young from harm, carefully hovering around the nest and gently arousing his children.

With such an awareness, one might sense the presence of God. This is actualised practically by the attitude of equanimity. Whether one finds praise or condemnation, whether things seem to work out or not, it is all the same. If it's good enough for God, it is good enough for me – that should be the attitude and like a slave to his master and a son to his father, one accepts whatever will be for He is the protective eagle. Whatever Hashem gives is good and something to work with in our service. The Ba'al Shem Tov describes the stage of equanimity to be a high level to attain.

יהוה בדד ינחנו ואין עמו אל נכר (5

"Hashem alone guided him, and there was no foreign god with him" (32:12).

"בדד" refers to being alone and yet with Hashem. This refers to our attitude in the world. We are to be part of the world, yet our mind should also seek beyond it; one should talk to Hashem in one's daily life. In this way, one may be free of idolatry, defined as anything one praises other than Hashem – be it false gods, lust, money and so on. In this way one can know God in all one's ways as it is famously put, so that one is both in this world and yet somehow not of this world. It also means connection to God is not something that is just recalled in shul, but in every domain of life. One has to use all one's gifts and talents in the service of God, so the Ba'al Shem Tov teaches.

"ינחנו" refers to giving tzedaka or charity and then one will be led in front of powerful people in both wealth and wisdom in order to sanctify God's name (Proverbs 18:16). The Rebbe in "Hayom Yom" writes/teaches that when someone gives of his efforts for the good endeavouring to spread the name of God, then Hashem helps miraculously and will widen one's perspective and put one in front of "great" and honoured people.

The last part of this sentence is the idea that one will come to a point in one's life where there will be no "yatza hara" (evil inclination) in both self and the world at large. In "Shemot" (Exodus 23:30) – מעת מעת קדשנו, expresses the idea Hashem is leading us in such a way that the bad will slowly fall away in a process that requires patience and work over time and then ultimately the darkness and evil shall be removed.

כי ידין יהוה עמו ועל עבדיו יתנחם כי יראה כי אזלת יד ואפס עצור ועזוב (6

"When Hashem will have carried out judgement upon His people, and regarding His servants, He shall reconsider, when He will see that the hand has gone, and there is none saved or emboldened" (32:36).

The name used to judge Israel is "Adonai" which is the aspect of mercy. Therefore, He will forgive his servants.

"Azlat" (אזלת) is gematria 438 which is equal to "galut" (exile)when the Kollel (the additional 1 for the word itself) is added. The letter yud follows and is equal in numerical value to Chabad (14) which is connected to mind and above the feelings. The idea is that in exile we are just surviving and don't usually have access to the higher faculties, the Chabad, in terms of awareness and higher mental understanding of God.

The following word (ואפס) means "nothing" and in this context refers to the power of the "sitra achra" (the negative side/force). Hashem places one in precarious situations so that one should find Him by calling to Him (the case of Jonah in the belly of the whale is interesting. He only called out to Hashem when he could not see a way out and was constrained on all sides). Whereas "azlat" above refers to deficiencies of the mind ("chabad"), this expression refers to the ability to control the emotions, the "middot" which is compromised in exile.

ועזוב is the sense of being left by Hashem. This is like judging one's fellow. Yet since every Jew has a Godly soul and emanates from Hashem Himself, one cannot stand in judgement from Above. In fact, it is taught that one who judges another judges himself. There is a story told by the prophet Natan in Shmual (2:12) of a rich man and a poor man and when a guest came to the former, he did not want to use of his own cattle, so he took the poor man's one sheep. King David was angered to hear such a story, but Natan reminded him that he is like the rich man in the story after his affair with Batsheva, since it is as if he stole from the poor man. Thus, it was King David's anger and judgement that was in fact a self-inflicted judgement. Thus, the Pirke Avot (Ethics of our fathers 1:6) reminds us to judge each person favourably and on the side of merit.

7) הרנינו גוים עמו כי דם עבדיו יקום ונקם ישיב לצריו וכפר אדמתו עמו

"Sing, nations, the praises of His people, for he will avenge the blood of His servants; he will bring retribution upon His enemies, and He will appease His land and His people" (32:43).

The prophesy is that ultimately the nations will praise Israel and Hashem will avenge all the calamities that befell Israel – the expulsions, the pogroms, the inquisition, the destruction of the temples, the crusades, the blood libel, the holocaust, the terrorism aimed at the new state and so on. Thus, all Israel's suffering, both psychological and physical will be avenged, while those who bless Israel and help Israel will themselves be blessed. The nations that do so will be part of the redemption and hasten it – they will be shepherds and farmers of the land (Isaiah 61:5). It Is quite simple – to hate the nation and people of Israel is to hate God, while using the gifts that has been bestowed on one whether it be wealth, talents, power and so on in order to help Israel will bring the redemption.

CHAPTER 10

VEZOT HA'BRACHA

וזאת הברכה אשר ברך משה איש האלהים ברך <u>משה איש האלהים</u> את בני ישראל לפני מותו (1

"And this is the blessing with which Moses the man of God blessed the Children of Israel before his death" (33:1).

What is "blessing"? When two Jews meet together, the customary way of greeting is for the one to say "shalom aleichem" and the other to respond in the exact opposite manner — "aleichem shalom". Even though these expressions would appear as one opposite the other, they in fact form a unity. In order for this to be achieved, one has to cultivate a soft heart. As Yecheskial says (36:26) — "I am going to take away the heart of stone and I am going to give you a heart of flesh". A "heart of flesh" *feels* in all its myriad ways in daily life, such as happiness, awe, love, fear, joy, mercy and so on. Fear itself strengthens love, for in any significant relationship, one ought to fear the loss of connection, the forestalling of a continued good relationship.

Furthermore, we bless each other by the proverbial "lechaim" ("to life!"). Unpacked the letters of that word denote other meanings. The "chet" is "chavush" or prison; the first "yud" is "yum" or sea (as in drowning); the second is "yesurim" or "illness" and the final "mem" is "midbar" or "desert". These are all negative aspects and the "lamed" as in "lechaim" denotes "lo" or "no" so that in effect we are blessing the other that he should be free of all such distresses and sufferings.

Now that it is specifically "Moshe, the man of God" (משה איש האלהים) that blesses us, so its power is magnified. The Ba'al Ha Turim writes that the first letters of that phrase spell "meah" or 100, while the lasts letters of the phrase spell "Moshe" or backwards "Hashem", "the name". The idea is that 100 refers to the completion of Moshe, that is, 10 sefirot within ten "sefirot", the harmony of the soul-powers. The 100 also refers to the 100 blessings one should say daily and it is this — as the Talmud explicates — that Hashem wants of us and connects us "Above".

תורה צוה לנו משה מורשה קהלת יעקב (2

"The Torah that Moses commanded us is the heritage of the Congregation of Jacob" (33:4).

This is indeed a very important line. In the Talmud (Sukkah 42:1) it says this is the first thing one teaches one's son, before even the "shema". Further in the Talmud (Baba Batra 14) it recounts that Rabbi Ami wrote 400 sefrei Torah in his life. Now this an impossible number to achieve in a lifetime. So, what could it mean? The Talmud resolves this by saying that in fact he wrote the line above 400 times. To write so many Torah's is unreasonable in one lifetime, but that if he wrote something he wrote this line, for this line is the essence of the Torah.

Torah has the numerical value of 611. These are the commandments given to Moshe to give to the Children of Israel. The additional 2 that comprise the full 613 Mitzvot are the first two commandments we all heard directly from God.

The idea here is that Torah is an "inheritance". Other than other fields of intellectual understanding, the Torah is a part of one's being. One can study the sciences or the arts and so on and yet it is still amalgamated to oneself, the knowledge is added and develops but is still essentially apart from he that learns it. The reason for this is that we learnt the whole Torah while in the womb and upon birth an angel strikes us on the lip and we forget it. Thus, when in this world we come to study the Torah, it is a kind of recall, our soul begins to remember what it once knew deeply (in fact Plato had the idea that true knowledge is a kind of remembrance).

Moreover, the three rings, so to speak that are bound together, are Torah, the nation of Israel and God. One can have a simple connection to God, like between a father and son, with no understanding, but a simple love, a love irrespective of abilities, effort and knowledge. However, one must also have a love wherein one looks into the Torah and learns what it is he has to do, for it is an instruction manual for life, not simply an abstract philosophy or a metaphysical treatise. It helps a person navigate his way in accordance with the laws and rules of existence in order to rise above matter or rather use it best.

ויהי בישרון מלך בהתאסף ראשי עם יחד שבטי ישראל (3

"And he became King over Jeshurun when the numbers of the nation are gathered – the tribes of Israel in unity" (33:5).

To experience God requires the unity of the Jewish people. There are many tribes of Israel, that is, unique expressions in language, culture, song, food and so on and these reflect different ways of connecting to God. Nevertheless, they are unified in following one set of Mitzvot. The idea of unity amidst diversity can be understood metaphorically in the discipline of art. Many colours all working together in correct proportion and intensity create harmony and even beauty. So too, the Jewish nation is like a body, a grand artwork, each aspect fulfilling its function and so long as there is harmony of parts, the "organism" as a whole and in detail survives and thrives.

In order for the above to be achieved one has to fulfil the mitzvah of loving a fellow Jew. In the sefer Tanya (chapter 32) the Rebbe speaks of such love and explains that to the extent one can engage in something one enjoys doing, that one's actual passions can be one's very livelihood and the way one spends one's days, then this is a kind of spiritual happiness and overrides purely material needs in that one's souls' desire is of paramount importance. To the extent one does this, one does not compare oneself to others or laments in envy that one should have a bigger house or a new car or whatever like so and so. Unity is brought about when we find this inner happiness and peace within by tapping into one's own joys, purpose and abilities.

To the extent that this can be done on a mass scale, so the various individuals and tribes of Israel fit like a puzzle and as all the pieces come together, so just like the body needs fuel and energy and light, so too the soul and in that oneness so a fully functioning organism with intelligence and love and free of blockages surfaces and then God blesses Israel.

האמר לאביו ולאמו לא ראיתיו ואת אחיו לא הכיר ואת בנו לא ידע כי שמרו אמרתך ובריתך ינצרו (4

"The one who said of his father and mother, 'I have not seen him'; his brother he did not recognize and his children he did not know" (33: 9).

The deeper layer of meaning of this verse is as follows: In a sense the road of one who wishes to return to the faith of Israel and follow in the ways of Torah and Mitzvot, must separate himself from all that he knew – in fact from one's family and the house of one's birth. A person who wishes to make the journey in effect is saying to his parents that he cannot accept their guidance; does not want to be like them – and this even extends to his brothers and son and daughter and wife. One leaves one's family to keep the Word of God and the covenant in order to get close to Hashem. Perhaps this is difficult, but it can be done with love and joy.

In order to be successful in coming close to God, what does one have to do? The Ba'al Shem Tov in the name of Saaidia Gaon, says that a person was created to break his bad nature.

 This call to leave all that one knew and to change his natural tendencies is echoed in the first book of the Torah, in "Bereishis", the portion of "Lech Lecha". In "Lech Lecha", Abraham is enjoined to leave his fathers house; his place of birth and land, which on deeper levels refers not simply to physically moving, but spiritually, so that one even cultivates one's thoughts, in the process departing from thought-structures (World-Views) and finding the path of Torah. In this sense, the reference in the "parsha" in "Bereishis" to "arzercha" is a code for will ("ratzon") and the reference to "moladecha" is to "nature" and "mebait avicha" is a reference to one's education – in all such instances one should change so that one is more soft and pure like the soul; she herself needing no "tikkun" ("fixing"), though she gets higher and higher. "Tikkun" is for the body and animal soul.

God promises Abraham that his name will be known as the world will be filled with Torah. It is one's will that can lead one to Hashem. Now Abraham, it is known, had ten trials. The first and probably the hardest was when he was thrown into the fire by Nimrod. But this trial is not in the 5 Books of the Torah and is found in more obscure sources and Midrashim. But the test of "Lech Lecha", the very name of the portion itself, is a test that we must all endure or rather resolutely take upon oneself. This may be more relevant to a returnee to Judaism (a Ba'al Teshuva), though every Jew needs to return to Hashem and leave aspects of his nature and environment which is counter-productive to that.

וימת שם משה עבד יהוה בארץ מואב <u>על פי יהוה</u> (5

"And Moses, servant of Hashem, died there, the land of Moab, by the mouth of Hashem" (34:5).

Here, at the end of Moses's life, some 120 years (he was 80 when God revealed Himself to him and the Shepherd of Israel for 40 years thereafter), the last part of the sentence ("al pi Hashem") comments Rashi is a reference to Hashem's "kissing" Moses. Moses returns to God as he passes so smoothly that two sentences later it says of Moses's death that his eyes did not dim so that even in his death, he continues to pray for Israel and bless Israel.

One could thus say that the righteous are alive even in their death. Insofar as their whole life that were doing their best to be one with the Torah and Mitzvot and the infinity, so upon death even the body itself goes higher; the body itself does not rot in the ground; death does not take hold and the body is eternal.

There is in fact a verified story that Rabbi Elimelech mi Lizensk, the brother of Reb Zushia of Anapoli, who lived a couple of centuries ago was buried in a town of Poland. The story is told of Nazis' who forced the Jews there to dig at the Rebbe's gravesight and when his body was exposed, it had not been defiled! The Nazis' ran in fear and the Jews were saved.

The purpose of the Torah and Mitzvot is to also elevate the body, along with the animal soul. Now, the order of existence from inanimate, to plant, to animal and to human is such that each raises up to the next, so where then does the human go? The human can get to the level of angels from the lowest part of angels called "ish" (person) and higher. There are 10 kinds/types of angels. When Yaakov in Bereishis 37:15 asked Josef to go and see how his brothers were doing, he lost his way and someone found him and directed him. Rashi comments that that "person" that found him was the angel Gabriel and Gabriel led him to his brothers.

ויהושע בן נון מלא רוח חכמה כי סמך משה את ידיו עליו וישמעו אליו בני ישראל ויעשו כאשר צוה (6 יהוה את משה

"Joshua son of Nun was filled with a spirit of wisdom, because Moses had laid his hands upon him, so that the Children of Israel obeyed him and did as Hashem had commanded Moses" (34:9).

If you read this line carefully, you might see that Israel accepted the new leader. Tradition teaches that Moses was like the face of the sun – burning, forever giving light – and Joshua is likened to the moon which reflects the light of the sun and is devoted. Now, an important principle is that Torah is not a history book; it applies to each generation. Therefore, we too need leaders and have leaders, shepherds like Moshe and the Patriarchs. Yet, now more than ever, Israel need a leader. As it says in Bamidbar (27:17): "…who shall go out before them, who shall take them out and who shall bring them in; and let the assembly of Hashem not be like sheep that have no shepherd". Who is this leader? What qualities does he have? The very next lines in the chapter of Devarim (i.e. 34:10) we are now analysing (in fact Torah is one, and any one point will lead to all other points) says that "he is a person with the spirit of God in him".

The Sages teach that this means he can get along with all types of people of the Nation of Israel, that he can relate to another; empathise and even in the great diversity of the people, he sees unity and reflects the other so that the other in turn finds his truth (It is said the Tzemach Tzeddik, the 3rd Lubavitcher Rebbe in answer to a student who asked why his message to him in public addresses was personal, that he, the Rebbe is but a maker of hats and sometimes various hats fit individual persons). A leader, a Rebbe could unify all differences.

ולכל היד החזקה ולכל המורא הגדול אשר עשה משה לעיני כל ישראל (7

"and for all the strong hand and for all the great awesomeness that Moses performed before the eyes of all Israel" (34:12).

This is the last sentence of the Torah. Moses was the ultimate prophet. Though we had prophets before, none was and none will be of the stature of Moses himself, not even the Mashiach. This is a basic principle in Judaism (c.f. Rambam's Thirteen Principles of Faith). To say he performed all this in front of the very eyes of the Children of Israel, means that each one of the people have a point of Moses within and it is this core that can help the individual to fear God; even the Talmud and the Tanya affirm that it is close for one to succeed in such a task. Even though, what is man really but a sack of blood and bones and sinews and so on; nevertheless one has to, as it were, have the "chutzpa" (audacity) to speak to Hashem just as the Breslov Rebbe taught, to activate that Moshe within of whom Rashi says that he could speak to Hashem anytime face to face, that is, inwardly and deeply in his conscious state.

Speaking is a massively interesting phenomenon. It says in Proverbs (12:25) that "Heaviness in the heart of man maketh it stoop, but a good word maketh it glad.". This points to the following: When a person has a problem, a worry, it is very good to speak to another as modern psychology knows only too well. The Rebbe says in HaYom Yom that it is good to speak to another that *cares about you* (not just anyone); or to distract one's mind (watch a movie, read a book, paint, shop – whatever) or thirdly, to speak to Hashem, for the Creator is one's father, friend, king and also one can learn Torah and through unifying with Hashem thereby enlighten and elevate the body, the self and the environment. Then, as Rashi says, one will be happy; one will have found the solution.

The last three words: "before the eyes of Israel" (see Hebrew Letters above) are such that the beginning letters of the three words are lamed (30), cuf (20) and yud (10) which spells the word "cli" meaning vessel. The final letter of each of the three words is yud (10), lamed (30), lamed (30) totalling 70, a reference to the nations of which there are 70 and Torah is a mechanism, a vessel for the Divine light which when enacted by a person which, brings the material to a higher plane, in turn uplifting the whole world. The vessel is the 620 Commandments of the Torah. It is the crown, the will (which also equals 620 – the Hebrew word for crown is keter – "cuf", "tuf", "reish". There are actually 620 Mitzvot, not 613, when we take into account the 7 commandments that were added by the sages after the time of Moses).

The importance of Israel then is crucial as the last Rashi on the Torah says that when Moses broke the tablets, he did the right thing, for the people are greater even than the Torah and that is why on Shabbat one can break the Torah to save a life or if one's wife is pregnant, the "Halachah" (the Way – Jewish law) is suspended to get one's wife safely to hospital.

When we finish reading a book of the Torah, we say "chazak, chazak vanitchazak" (Be strong! Be strong! And may we be strengthened!). Three chazak's (chet (8), zayin (7) and kuf (100)) total 345, the numerical equivalent (gematria) of Moshe (mem (40, shin (300) an heh (5)).

We are strengthened to ascend to Hashem. He is like a burning fire, an intense light that none can bear. Coming too close would surely consume one! The last point here is that one should be strengthened with the vessel, the Torah and Mitzvot, in which the light can find a steady diffusion, a home, and steady expansion over time. Thus the Talmud says that one can indeed approach Hashem and this is done by doing the Mitzvot, those strands of light-energy that can connect one Above (and yes, we can understand their significance, their mystical source, but they are of the will and transcend wisdom, understanding and knowledge).

CONCLUTION:

The beginning of the Torah is a "Bet". The last letter is a "lamed". Together they are "lev" or heart. The heart, an energy-centre that pumps blood to all parts of the body, a muscle activated even if the brain does not activate it. It is a muscle of enormous power; it is the seat of love and the emotions. The heart's expression follows the dictates of thought. It is thus the king ruling either wisely or the reverse over the body, the chariot.

This little book are just some reflections on the book of Devarim. There are obviously countless other commentaries on the sentences chosen and still yet further commentaries on every line of Torah, on the relationship between sentences and paragraphs, between portions themselves, in terms of the book as a whole, in relation to the other four books and in terms of the whole corpus of Torah – Nach (prophets and writings), Talmud, Kabbalah and Chassidus, though the slant of this book is generally gleaned from the Chabad Rebbeim and Chassidus, though Rashi also appears frequently.

In any which way it is to be perceived, Torah is unitary. At the same time, it is written that you can find wisdom in other cultures, but all the wisdoms of the world can be found in Torah, for Torah is divine. Each of the 7 points enumerated are "little gems" and in their finitude they are part of the unity of the Torah and therefore essentially infinite applying to all times and mores.

It is the authors' sincere hope that this has at least ignited or confirmed the reader's spiritual intuitions and thoughts, it is but the surface, the tip of the iceberg, at the same time every limitation, even the size of Plank's Constant, contains the universal as a famous poet once said something akin to this – to see eternity in an hour and infinity in a grain of sand.

Finally, the Alter Rebbe, Rav Shneur Zalman of Liadi, the first Rebbe of Chabad, gave an order to live with the parsha of the week, the part that we read every week and the part that pertains to a particular day of the week. The second order was that Moshe Rebbeinu was ordered to make a snake to combat the many snakes that came in the desert and attacked the people. Moses's snake was made from copper, because "nachash" or snake and "nachoshet" (copper) (Bamidbar 27:9) sounds the same. The former is a code for the "weekday", while the latter is that of "shabbat" (The 7th - "sheva") and so in order to show that he has love for God all aspects of the weekday should be infused with shabbat. The third order then is to remember the shabbat to keep it. To combine these orders – to live with the parsha of the week and to do it in a special way are connected with shabbat – the 7, the 7000's age – which is to say the formation of a better world, an era of Shabbas. In other words, the very days of the week and shabbat are one and related, so that ultimately there will just be shabbat – joy, rest, peace and wisdom.

ABOUT THE AUTHORS

Moshe Guy is a sofer stam (scribe) and lives in Haifa, Israel. For any comments and questions, please contact Moshe at: 972 52 669 4770 (available on whatsupp) and mosheguybursh on facebook

Daniel Shorkend holds a doctorate in art history and is a practicing artist and teacher. For any comments and questions contact Daniel at: drshokend@gmail.com

Printed by Books on Demand GmbH, Norderstedt / Germany